FOREVER PRESENT

The Unbreakable Bonds
We Share with Our Pets

ARWIN VALENCIA, MD

Copyright Notice

Copyright © 2025 by ANG Power Publishing House.
All Rights Reserved.

No part of this publication, including but not limited to Forever Present: The Unbreakable Bonds We Share with Our Pets, may be reproduced, stored in a database or retrieval system, or distributed, or transmitted in any form or by any means, including photocopying, recording, or other electronic or mechanical methods, without the prior written permission of the copyright holder, except in the case of brief quotations embodied in critical reviews and certain other noncommercial uses permitted by copyright law. For permission requests, write to the copyright holder at the address below.

> ANG POWER PUBLISHING HOUSE
> PO BOX 10735 / Glendale, CA 91209-USA
> ANGPowerPHouse@Gmail.com
> ISBN: 978-1-966837-40-4

This publication contains proprietary information pertaining to Forever Present: The Unbreakable Bonds We Share with Our Pets. Unauthorized use, duplication, or adaptation of the concepts, graphics, or other materials within is strictly prohibited and punishable under applicable laws.

Disclaimer: The author and publisher have made every effort to ensure the accuracy of the information in this publication. However, they assume no responsibility for errors or omissions or for any consequences resulting from the use of the information provided. This book is intended for educational and informational purposes only and does not constitute professional or legal advice.

All trademarks, service marks, product names, and logos referenced in this book are the property of their respective owners. Forever Present: The Unbreakable Bonds We Share with Our Pets is the intellectual property of Arwin Valencia, MD and is protected under copyright law.

First Edition - Printed in the United States of America

Table of Contents

Introduction...1
Part I: The Sacred Bond 9
Chapter 1: Companions of the Soul...11
The Gift of Animal Companionship...11
Chapter 2: The Language of Unconditional Love..................21
Love Without Judgment...22
Chapter 3: Animal Angels Companions Beyond the Seen....32
Part II: Beyond the Veil...42
Chapter 4: Echoes of Eternity - The Invisible Thread of Love..........44
Chapter 5: The Continuum of Life..53
The Great Circle of Being...54
Chapter 6: Signs from Spirit Companions...............................63
When Love Learns a New Language...64
Part III: Walking Through Grief..80
Chapter 7: The Human Heart and the Void............................82
When Love Leaves Footprints in Silence..................................82
Chapter 8: Healing in Silence and Expression.........................96
The White Coat and the Cracked Heart...................................96
Chapter 9: Coco's Story - Grief in Those Left Behind..........111
I Am Still Here..111
Chapter 10: Soul Companions Forever 121
Love That Does Not End...121
Chapter 11: The Cosmic Ark - The Old Story Sailing..........130
into the Future...130
Chapter 12: Forever Present - The Eternal Echo of Love....142
Epilogue: The Eternal Echo..150
The Blessing of Companionship Beyond Time.....................151
Benediction for Cody and Chloe - -*MysticSojourn66*- 153
About the Author..**155**

Dedication

To Chloe and Cody,

Our beloved angelic companions who walked beside us for nearly eighteen years.
Your love was unconditional, your loyalty unshaken, your presence a constant grace.
Though you have crossed into eternity, your pawprints remain etched forever in our souls.

And to Coco,

the joyful spirit still here with us, carrying the light of her siblings,
reminding us of each day that love continues, unbroken and alive.

This book is for you,

for the laughter you gave, the comfort you offered,
and the eternal truth you revealed:
love never dies, it only transforms.

Forever Present

-MysticSojourn66-

They came with fur, yet wings unseen,
Messengers of love, both pure and keen.
With every gaze, with every sigh,
They taught us truths no gold could buy.

No judgment cast, no grudges kept,
They stayed beside us while we wept.
Their hearts were open, vast, and wide,
A living echo of God inside.

Now silence lingers where paws once tread,
Yet love still sings though tears are shed.
For bonds of spirit never sever,
What love has joined remains forever.

So, when the night feels cold, alone,
We listen deep — We hear their tone.
Not gone, not lost, just changed in view,
Forever present, forever true.

Introduction

Pets are among the greatest gifts that the Divine bestows upon us in this earthly construct. Their presence is a grace, woven into the fabric of our daily lives to remind us that love, in its purest form, requires no conditions. In the constant tide of life's ups and downs—its challenges, anxieties, and uncertainties—a true companion does not merely walk alongside us but holds us steady when the ground feels like it is crumbling beneath our feet.

What is a companion in the truest sense? It is not only someone who shares our days, but someone who remains when storms rise. A companion is one who does not keep score, who does not judge, who does not withdraw love when we falter or fail. Our pets embody this kind of companionship more completely than most humans can. They forgive instantly. They see us not through the fog of our imperfections, but with eyes filled only with recognition:

You are mine, and I am yours.

There is something disarming, even humbling, in this. When I return home exhausted, distracted by the weight of the NICU load or consumed by life's endless demands, there they are—tails wagging, eyes bright, waiting only to love and be loved. Their joy is contagious. Their silent comfort dissolves sorrows. In their small, furry bodies lies an infinite reservoir of presence.

What do they ask in return? Almost nothing. Food, shelter, gentle touch, the routine of daily walks. A safe place to belong. For so little, they offer us everything. And so I cannot see dogs as merely animals. I see them as emissaries of the angelic realm—angels disguised in fur, wings hidden yet always outstretched, lifting us higher into consciousness with each act of unconditional devotion.

But in the rush of daily life, how often do we forget? Entangled in our dramas and distracted by the noise of this material world, we sometimes neglect them. We get irritated when they bark at the wrong time, impatient when they ask for attention, blind to their silent pleas when we are consumed by our own troubles. And still, they forgive. Still, they remain. Until the day comes when their earthly journey closes, and we are left to face the unbearable silence of their absence.

The grief that follows is unlike any other. The void they leave is not abstract; it is palpable, as though a great chasm has been carved into the heart. You feel it when you walk past their empty bed, when you reach for the leash that no longer has a purpose, when the sound of silence echoes louder than any noise. It is a wound that time alone does not heal.

I know this grief well.

I was blessed with two extraordinary Coton de Tulear companions, Chloe and Cody, who lived alongside me for nearly eighteen years. Chloe, with her gentle spirit, crossed the rainbow bridge in October of last year. Cody, with his loyal heart, followed her eleven months later, this past September. Their departures came like twin waves crashing against the fragile walls of my soul. Just as my heart began to heal from Chloe's passing, Cody's absence tore it open again.

I cannot easily put into words the magnitude of the loss. They were not simply pets; they were my children. They were the ones who made my house a home, who filled it with laughter, warmth, and unconditional love. They were woven into the very rhythm of my days and the intimacy of my nights. Every small routine—from waking in the morning to resting in the evening—was punctuated by their presence.

Without them, the house feels quieter, emptier. Even with my husband and sister by my side, even with our youngest Coton, Coco, still here with us, the energy has shifted. Coco, only eight years old, lived every day of her life with her two siblings. I see in her the confusion of their absence. She searches for them, sniffing their old places, her eyes carrying a question she cannot put into words. Perhaps she too grieves. Or perhaps she feels what I feel but cannot explain: that they are here and not here, visible and invisible, shifted into a realm just beyond perception.

For me, grief arrives as silence. I choose to mourn privately, to internalize. It is not in my nature to display the fullness of my sorrow outwardly. In my profession as a neonatologist, I was trained to compartmentalize—to separate feeling from action, to focus only on what must be done when a newborn arrives not breathing, when life and death hang in the balance. There is no room for hesitation in such moments. The heart must be still, emotions repressed, so that hands may act swiftly and decisively.

But what happens to those emotions, pressed down day after day, year after year? They embed themselves deeply into the psyche, sinking into the body, surfacing later as unexplained fatigue, as pain, as illness. And so, when my beloved Chloe and Cody left me, I found that my grief was not easily expressed, yet neither could it be easily contained. It stretched long and heavy inside me, weaving itself into my days like a shadow I could not shake.

Yet, even within this pain, I feel gratitude. These two angelic beings entered my life exactly when I needed them most. They were not accidents of circumstance. I believe, with all my heart, that souls choose their companions, and companions choose their souls. Chloe and Cody were soul contracts—agreements made beyond time—that they would walk beside me in this life; to teach me lessons I could not learn any other way.

Caring for them was not always effortless. It required energy, patience, discipline. But the love and joy they gave in return surpassed every challenge. In their eyes, I learned to see myself more clearly. In their devotion, I recognized the reflection of Divine Love. In their quirks, antics, and playful spirits, I found healing for the fragmented parts of my own soul. They became my children, my guardians, my teachers.

Their departure has left me broken, but not shattered. Broken in a way that allows the light to seep in. Broken so that love may expand. The truth is that sometimes the heart must crack open for the light within to shine forth.

The journey for those of us left behind must continue. Life insists upon itself. And yet, I walk with the quiet certainty that Chloe and Cody are not gone. They have only shifted dimensions, crossing into a realm where their love is not diminished but magnified. They continue to watch, to guide, to remain.

I feel them in the quiet moments when I sit in stillness. I dream of them, their presence vivid, as if they had simply curled up beside me once again. I sense them in subtle ways—a flicker of movement at the edge of my vision, a memory that arrives unbidden but feels alive. These are not coincidences; they are echoes of eternity.

For those who have been touched by such companions, life is never the same. Once you have been loved by a pet, you cannot return to who you were before. You are changed. You have glimpsed a form of love that mirrors Divine Source itself—love that is faithful, forgiving, constant, and pure. This love reshapes us, molds us, stretches our hearts into something larger, something softer, something truer.

And so, while their bodies may no longer be here, their essence remains. Love does not vanish. Love transforms. Chloe and Cody are still near, their pawprints etched into the fabric of my soul. They are part of the eternal continuum, woven into the quantum web of existence where no bond is ever severed.

This, perhaps, is the deeper truth that I hope to share through this book: that the bonds we share with our pets are not temporary. They are mystical and eternal, stretching beyond the limits of time and space. Science now hints at what mystics have always known—that all beings are connected by threads of energy, that once entangled, two souls are forever linked. Pets and humans are no exception.

From the perspective of spirit, Chloe and Cody are still here, and always will be. Their love remains alive, pulsing in every memory, every tear, every laugh I recall at their antics. They are woven into my being in ways words cannot fully capture. And when my own time comes to cross the veil, I trust that they will be there, waiting—not as memories, but as luminous beings of love.

Until then, my journey continues. I carry them with me, I thank them for the gift of their lives, and I allow their love to shape me into a more compassionate, patient, and open-hearted human being. For I can truly say: I am who I am today because of my sweet Chloe and Cody.

To them I say, with all the love my heart can hold:

Thank you. Thank you for every wag of your tail, every look in your eyes, every moment of unconditional devotion. Thank you for healing me, for teaching me, for walking beside me.

You are not gone.
You are forever present.
You are forever mine.
You are forever light.

Part I

The Sacred Bond

Chapter 1:
Companions of the Soul
The Gift of Animal Companionship

From the dawn of human memory, pets have stood beside us as companions, protectors, and teachers. They are more than mere animals in our homes; they are emissaries of love, reflections of loyalty, and silent witnesses to our joys and sorrows. For many, a pet embodies a living, breathing expression of divine grace. Their loyalty, affection, and ability to forgive unconditionally remind us of God's own boundless love—a love that accepts us not for what we do, but simply for who we are.

To love a pet is to step into a relationship untainted by the complexities that often accompany human interactions. Their affection is not contingent on our status, wealth, or achievements. They do not hold grudges when we falter or fail. Instead, their companionship is steady and unrelenting, offering us a mirror of the love that, in the deepest spiritual sense, already surrounds us.

In the quiet presence of a dog resting at our feet, the purring of a cat curled on our lap, or the melodic chatter of a parrot at dawn, we are reminded that companionship can be simple, direct, and deeply healing. Pets are not distractions from life's greater journey; they are fellow travelers on the soul's pilgrimage, nudging us toward presence, humility, and love.

How Pets Embody Divine Love

Unconditional Love and Acceptance

Perhaps the most striking quality of pets is their unconditional love. A dog leaps with joy when its owner returns home, even if only minutes have passed. A cat may quietly settle beside its human after a difficult day, wordlessly offering comfort. These gestures are small, yet they reveal a profound truth: love does not demand perfection. It thrives in presence, forgiveness, and simple togetherness.

For many, this kind of love feels divine. It mirrors the biblical promise that God loves humanity not for its achievements or worthiness, but because love is God's very nature. Pets, in their simplicity, make this truth visible.

Loyalty and Devotion

The steadfast loyalty of pets is legendary. Dogs, in particular, have long been celebrated for their faithfulness.

They guard, follow, and remain present even in times of difficulty. Their devotion stirs within us an awareness of what loyalty means in our relationship with the Divine. Just as pets remain by our side, God's presence remains constant, even when we stray or forget.

Joy and Presence

Animals live fully in the present moment. They do not ruminate about yesterday's mistakes or fret about tomorrow's uncertainties. A dog chasing a ball, a bird singing at sunrise, or a cat stretching in the warmth of the sun all embody a sacred truth: joy arises from presence. Their example encourages us to release our anxious grasp on time and rediscover the divine gift of "now."

Spiritual Companionship

For many, a pet's presence is more than comforting—it is spiritual. They sit beside us in prayer, listen in silence to our whispered griefs, and walk with us in our seasons of solitude. Their companionship reminds us that we are never alone, echoing the assurance that God, too, is always near.

Religious and Cultural Perspectives

Across religions and cultures, animals have been revered not only as companions but as spiritual symbols.

Christianity: Pets are often seen as gifts from God, teaching lessons of love, humility, and trust. The joy and loyalty of animals echo the fruits of the Spirit.

Judaism: Pets are considered beloved members of the family, reflecting the Jewish emphasis on kindness toward all creatures (**tza'ar ba'alei chayim**).

Hinduism: Krishna's playful affection for animals, especially cows and dogs, highlights the sacred bond between humans and creation.

Sufism (Islamic Mysticism): The dog is revered as a symbol of humility and devotion, embodying the soul's longing for God.

Ancient Civilizations: Egyptians venerated cats as divine protectors, while Anubis, the jackal-headed god, guided souls to the afterlife. In Greek mythology, dogs often appear as faithful companions or guides to the underworld.

These perspectives reveal a universal truth: animals are not spiritually neutral. They are participants in the cosmic dance, messengers of wisdom, and symbols of truths too profound for words.

Pets as Spiritual Teachers

If we are attentive, pets can become our spiritual teachers.

Modeling Love

A pet's affection offers us a living lesson in how to love without condition. They teach us to give love freely, without calculation or expectation.

Teaching Forgiveness

Pets forgive with astonishing ease. Even when neglected or scolded, they return with trust. Their forgiveness is not weakness; it is strength born of love. For humans struggling with resentment, this example becomes a powerful call to let go.

Inspiring Faith

In their quiet companionship, pets often deepen our awareness of God's presence. Their loyalty and simplicity point us to the same qualities in the Divine. They remind us that love, joy, and devotion are not luxuries but essential elements of spiritual life.

Evolutionary Partnership

The human-pet bond is not merely emotional; it is deeply

rooted in history and evolution.

Dogs: Descended from wolves more than 15,000 years ago, dogs entered human life as allies in hunting and protection. Their loyalty was forged in the crucible of survival.

Cats: Around 10,000 years ago, cats were drawn to human settlements by the promise of food. Over time, they evolved from aloof hunters to cherished companions.

Other Animals: Horses, birds, and even small rodents have played roles in human companionship, each forming unique bonds with their caretakers.

This partnership has shaped both species, creating a bond that is not only emotional but biological.

The Biology of Bonding

Modern science confirms what we feel in our hearts: pets and humans share a neurochemical bond. When we interact with pets—stroking their fur, gazing into their eyes, or simply being near them—both human and animal brains release oxytocin, the "love hormone."

This biochemical exchange reduces stress, lowers blood pressure, and fosters feelings of safety and belonging. It is no wonder that pets are increasingly recognized as therapeutic partners, offering healing through presence alone.

Loyalty in Myth and Symbol

Throughout history, pets—especially dogs and cats—have been enshrined in stories of loyalty, guidance, and protection.

Greek Mythology: Argos, the loyal dog of Odysseus, recognized his master after 20 years of absence and died content, embodying fidelity.

Aztec Tradition: Xolotl, the dog-headed deity, guided souls through the underworld.

Egyptian Mythology: Anubis, with the head of a jackal, was the guardian of the dead. Cats, revered as sacred, were associated with Bastet, goddess of home and protection.

Chinese Tradition: Guardian lions, often called "Foo Dogs," symbolize protection and loyalty, stationed at temple gates.

These myths reveal a consistent truth: humanity has long perceived animals as sacred symbols of loyalty, protection, and spiritual guidance.

Pets as Ideal Friends in Modern Times

Today, pets embody the archetype of the "ideal friend."

Non-Judgmental Support: Unlike human relationships, pets do not judge. They accept us as we are.

Emotional Anchors: Pets provide stability in times of distress, easing anxiety and offering comfort.

Simple Joys: From the wag of a tail to the warmth of a curled body on the couch, pets remind us that joy need not be complex.

This simplicity is precisely why their companionship feels so healing.

How Pets Love Differently

Each species, and indeed each individual pet, loves in its own way.

Dogs: Express affection overtly—through loyalty, play, and protective behavior.

Cats: Demonstrate love with subtlety—through purring, kneading, or simply choosing to share space.

Parrots: Bond through vocalization, mimicry, and companionship, though their unique biology shapes how they show affection.

Beyond species, individual experiences shape a pet's attachment style. Rescue animals, for instance, may show wariness at first but often grow into profound loyalty when given consistent love.

The Human-Pet Dynamic

Ultimately, the human-pet relationship is one of mutual dependence. Humans provide safety, food, and shelter. Pets, in return, provide affection, companionship, and spiritual lessons. Yet this dynamic is not transactional. It is a relationship of love that enriches both lives.

Humans often project their emotions onto pets, interpreting their behaviors as signs of affection. Yet even when filtered through projection, the truth remains: pets foster within us the capacity for compassion, patience, and selfless love.

Reflective Summary

Pets are not accidental presences in our lives; they are soul-companions and teachers. Their unconditional love reflects divine love. Their loyalty mirrors God's constancy. Their joy in the present moment teaches us to let go of anxiety and dwell in gratitude. Across cultures and religions, they have been honored as sacred beings, guides to the afterlife, and symbols of fidelity.

From the evolutionary campfires of ancient humans to the modern living room, pets have walked beside us as friends, protectors, and spiritual mirrors. Their presence grounds us, heals us, and elevates us toward greater compassion.

In truth, to love a pet is to glimpse the eternal love that sustains all creation.

Meditative Reflections

1. Presence: Close your eyes and imagine your pet (or a beloved animal you once knew) beside you. Feel their steady presence. Allow yourself to rest in this moment without judgment.

2. Unconditional Love: Reflect on how your pet loves you without condition. Can you extend this kind of love to yourself and others today?

3. Forgiveness: Recall a time when your pet forgave you quickly and returned with love. In silence, ask yourself: whom do I need to forgive?

4. Gratitude: Place your hand over your heart and whisper gratitude for the companionship of animals. Thank God for sending them as reflections of His boundless love.

5. Union with the Divine: Imagine that every wag of a tail, every purr, every chirp, is a whisper from the Divine, reminding you: You are loved. You are never alone.

Chapter 2: The Language of Unconditional Love
Love Without Judgment

Unconditional love is a phrase often used to describe the highest form of affection—a love that does not calculate worth, keep score, or place conditions on being received. For many people, this kind of love is elusive in human relationships, where judgments, expectations, and disappointments can cloud affection. Yet in the presence of pets, unconditional love is not a theory; it is an everyday reality.

Pets love without judgment. They do not care about how successful we are, how many mistakes we've made, or whether we've lived up to society's ideals. They accept us in our rawness—in our joy, in our sorrow, and even in our flaws. Their consistent loyalty and presence cut through the noise of our imperfections and remind us that at the core of being, we are worthy of love simply because we exist.

This kind of love is transformative because it creates a safe emotional environment where the heart can rest. For many, the companionship of a pet is not just soothing—it is healing. It allows a person to feel seen and cherished without condition, echoing the eternal love of the Divine.

Characteristics of Non-Judgmental Love

Acceptance Without Conditions

At the heart of a pet's love is acceptance. A dog does not care whether you are wealthy or poor, fashionable or plain, eloquent or awkward. A cat does not measure your worth by your achievements. They love you as you are—unadorned and unmasked.

In this acceptance, there is a spiritual lesson. Pets remind us that the essence of love lies not in evaluation but in being fully present to another. They invite us to accept ourselves with the same unconditional openness they so freely extend.

Loyalty and Companionship

Pets embody steadfast loyalty. They remain by their owner's side in times of joy and sorrow, triumph and failure. Their companionship mirrors the biblical ideal of faithfulness, of walking beside another no matter the circumstances. In this way, pets model what it means to be a true companion—one who does not leave when life becomes difficult.

Forgiveness and Lack of Grudges

Perhaps one of the most striking qualities of pets is their ability to forgive. A dog may be scolded harshly but, moments later, returns with wagging tail and open heart. A cat may experience neglect yet still curl up to sleep beside the one who failed them. Their forgiveness is not naive—it is instinctive, flowing from their capacity to remain rooted in love.

This quality challenges us as humans, who so often hold onto resentment and grudges. Pets reveal that forgiveness is not weakness but strength, a decision to love beyond the wounds.

Focus on the Present

While humans are prone to living in the past or the future—regretting what has been or worrying about what might come—pets live fully in the present. Their joy in the moment is contagious: a dog celebrating a walk as though it is the grandest adventure, a cat delighting in a patch of sunlight as if it were a priceless treasure. Pets are natural teachers of mindfulness.

Unconditional Support

Pets create a secure space where people feel loved and supported. They provide comfort during difficult times without demanding explanations. In their quiet companionship, they remind us of God's promise never to abandon us.

How Pets Show Their Love

Love, for pets, is often expressed not in words but in actions. Their gestures are small yet profound, communicating affection in ways that touch the soul.

Physical Affection: A dog licking a face, a cat kneading with its paws, or a bird preening gently are acts of intimacy. These gestures reassure us that love is alive and near.

Greeting and Proximity: The excitement of a dog running to meet its owner at the door, the quiet persistence of a cat following from room to room, or the chatter of a parrot seeking attention are expressions of belonging. Pets want to be close.

Emotional Support: Animals are sensitive to human emotions. A dog will rest its head on your lap when you cry;

a cat may sit silently beside you during grief. Their intuition is a gift of healing presence.

A Sense of Purpose: Caring for a pet provides humans with a sense of meaning. Feeding, walking, grooming, and protecting them nurtures a sense of responsibility and importance, which in turn enriches the human spirit.

The Pet as a Mirror

One of the most profound aspects of the human-animal bond is the way pets act as mirrors. They reflect back to us aspects of ourselves that we may not easily see.

Reflecting Our Inner Self: Pets often mirror our moods and energy. An anxious person may notice their pet becoming restless, while a calm demeanor in the human often elicits calmness in the pet. In this reflection, we see our inner state more clearly.

The Mirror of Unconditional Love: A pet's unwavering devotion reflects back our own best qualities. Their love reveals to us the capacity for gentleness, patience, and kindness that lives within us.

Highlighting a Shared Life: Looking at old photos or videos of a pet reveals not only their story but ours. The memories we share with them become reflections of the life we built together, a testimony to shared love and growth.

Grief, Reflection, and Healing

The death of a beloved pet is devastating because it feels like losing a piece of our heart. Their absence is felt not only in the empty spaces they leave behind but also in the missing reflection of love they once provided.

Reflection as a Healing Practice

Journaling: Writing about memories, lessons learned, and the impact of a pet can transform grief into gratitude.

Creating a Memorial: A small altar with photos, toys, or collars provides a sacred space to honor their memory.

Writing a Letter: Expressing unspoken love or regrets in a letter to a pet can bring closure.

Volunteering: Honoring a pet's legacy through acts of kindness to other animals creates a ripple of love that transcends death.

Mirrors in Cultural Grieving Traditions

In Judaism, mirrors are covered during shiva to invite inward reflection, symbolizing the need to focus on loss and healing.

In folklore, mirrors were sometimes covered to release the spirit of the deceased, ensuring it would not be trapped. This offers a metaphor for allowing grief to flow, rather than imprisoning love in sorrow.

In Eastern traditions, the mirror symbolizes impermanence. Covering it acknowledges the transient nature of life, while affirming that memory and love remain eternal.

Pets, as mirrors, remind us that though their physical presence fades, their love lives on in our hearts.

The Quiet Wisdom of Patience

Pets teach patience not through words but through their being.

Waiting Without Worry: A dog patiently waiting for a walk demonstrates trust that its needs will be met.

The Art of Slow: Pets savor life—sniffing the air, pausing to play, basking in sunlight. Their slowness teaches us to notice the sacred in ordinary moments.

Growth Through Process: Training a pet requires patience, consistency, and grace. Through this process, we learn that mistakes are not failures but stepping stones to growth.

The Gentle Practice of Presence

In a distracted world, pets are anchors of presence.

Masters of the "Here and Now": Pets do not dwell on past pain or worry about the future. They live in the present moment, reminding us to do the same.

Finding Joy in Simplicity: A simple toy, a walk, or a patch of sunshine is enough to delight them. Their joy teaches us that happiness is found not in excess but in appreciation.

Natural Reset Buttons: When a pet nudges us for attention, they call us back from our screens and our stress to the sacred moment at hand.

Communication Beyond Words: The silent understanding shared in a look or touch with a pet reminds us that love transcends language.

Cultivating a Deeper Bond

The lessons of unconditional love, forgiveness, patience, and presence not only deepen our relationship with pets but enrich our lives as a whole. Engaging intentionally with these lessons makes us more empathetic, more grounded, and more capable of love.

Pets remind us that love does not need to be earned—it is simply given. In their companionship, we learn to mirror that love in our own relationships and in our spiritual journey.

Reflective Summary

The language of unconditional love is spoken fluently by pets. It is a language of acceptance without conditions, loyalty without limits, forgiveness without hesitation, and presence without distraction. Their love is a mirror that reveals to us our best selves, while also teaching us how to forgive, how to wait, and how to live in the sacredness of the present.

When pets leave us, the grief is profound because we lose not only a companion but also a mirror of divine love. Yet their memory continues to teach, comfort, and guide us. Through reflective practices, we transform grief into gratitude and continue their legacy of unconditional love.

To walk with a pet is to walk with a teacher of the soul, one who speaks in silence, heals with presence, and loves without end.

Meditative Reflections

1. Mirror Meditation: Sit in silence and recall how your pet mirrored your moods, your joy, or your love. What qualities of yourself did they bring forward that you might nurture now?

2. Unconditional Love Exercise: Close your eyes and visualize your pet's gaze of unconditional love. Imagine God looking at you with the same gaze. Let yourself rest in that acceptance.

3. Forgiveness Practice: Recall a moment when your pet forgave you easily. Breathe deeply and ask yourself: Who in my life needs this kind of forgiveness from me?

4. Presence Practice: Spend five minutes observing your surroundings as though you were a pet—notice small details, sounds, and sensations. Rest in the simplicity of the moment.

5. Gratitude Ritual: Whisper a thank you to your pet, whether living or passed on. Acknowledge the lessons of love they taught you. Feel their presence as a blessing that continues to shape your life.

Chapter 3: Animal Angels Companions Beyond the Seen

Across cultures and through centuries, humans have looked to the animal kingdom not only for survival but for spiritual guidance. Animals have been revered as messengers, guardians, healers, and allies—bridging the gap between the visible and invisible realms. In the quiet gaze of an owl, the fierce loyalty of a wolf, or the playful leap of a dolphin, people have sensed divine wisdom. Pets and wild animals alike have been understood as animal angels, earthly beings carrying heavenly messages, embodying virtues, and guiding souls toward growth.

In our homes today, pets may seem like ordinary companions—dogs lounging on couches, cats curled in sunbeams—but their role is often far deeper. For many, these animals are spiritual teachers in disguise, partners in soul contracts, and angels cloaked in fur, feathers, or scales. Their presence reassures us that divine guidance

is not reserved for lofty visions—it can be found in the wag of a tail, the nuzzle of a nose, or the patient gaze of eyes that see straight into the heart.

Indigenous and Shamanic Traditions

Many Indigenous cultures hold profound respect for animals, seeing them as spiritual kin and guides.

Spirit Animals and Totems

Among Native American peoples, spirit animals or totems embody specific traits that individuals or tribes draw upon for guidance. The eagle soars high, symbolizing vision, freedom, and divine perspective. The wolf exemplifies loyalty, intuition, and teamwork. The bear reflects strength and introspection, retreating into hibernation as a metaphor for turning inward during times of transformation.

Totems are not abstract symbols; they are living, breathing companions on the spiritual path. In ceremonies, dreams, and visions, these animals appear to offer wisdom precisely when it is most needed.

Intermediaries and Healers

Shamans often work with animal spirits as intermediaries between the human and spiritual worlds. In rituals, drumming journeys, or vision quests, animals arrive as guides—offering protection, messages, and healing. A jaguar may appear to teach courage; a snake may come to symbolize rebirth and shedding of old ways.

Cultural Connection

For Indigenous communities, animals are woven into the very fabric of creation stories. They are not separate from humanity but part of a vast interconnected web of life. To honor animals as spiritual guides is to honor the entire natural universe as sacred.

Hawaiian Lore: 'Aumakua

In Hawaiian tradition, the 'aumakua are family guardians who often take the form of animals—sharks, owls, turtles, or even dogs. An 'aumakua is more than a symbol; it is believed to be the spirit of an ancestor who continues to protect and guide the family.

For Hawaiians, encountering one's 'aumakua in the natural world is a sacred moment—a sign of connection, reassurance, and wisdom. It reminds families that their lineage is not severed by death but continues in protective presence. Pets, too, are sometimes regarded as embodiments of 'aumakua, living reminders of ancestral love.

Symbolic Roles of Animal Angels

Messengers and Protectors

In countless traditions, animals appear as messengers of the divine. A bird flying across one's path at a significant moment may be interpreted as a sign. A dog's sudden alertness or a cat's focused gaze can feel like warnings or reassurances. These messengers often arrive at pivotal times—moments of grief, transition, or decision—reminding us that unseen help is near.

Dream Guides

Animals also appear in dreams as guides. A horse galloping across dream landscapes may symbolize newfound freedom or power. A snake may signal transformation. A butterfly often represents the soul or spiritual rebirth. Such dreams are often understood as communications from the subconscious or the spiritual world, delivered through animal imagery.

Embodiments of Virtue

Each animal embodies virtues humans can emulate. The wolf's loyalty, the dove's peace, the lion's courage, and the deer's gentleness all become living metaphors. By observing or connecting with animals, humans are reminded of the virtues they are called to cultivate within themselves.

Examples Across Traditions

North America: The Lakota people honored animals as conduits to universal power, calling upon them through chants and ceremonies for healing and good fortune.

Ancient Egypt: The crocodile embodied both danger and protection, represented in the god Sobek, who guarded against evil and symbolized fertility. Cats, as manifestations of Bastet, were protectors of home and hearth.

Norse Mythology: The monstrous dog Garmr guarded the gates of Hel, protecting the threshold between the living and the dead. Ravens, associated with Odin, symbolized wisdom and prophecy.

These examples highlight a global truth: animals are not merely creatures of instinct but bearers of mystery, symbolic carriers of divine energy.

Soul Contracts with Pets

Beyond cultural traditions, many spiritual seekers today speak of soul contracts with their pets—agreements made before birth between souls, human and animal, to walk together in this life.

The Purpose of Soul Contracts

Teaching Lessons: Pets embody unconditional love, patience, and presence, becoming masters who guide humans into deeper compassion.

Healing and Mirroring: Pets often absorb and transmute their human's negative energy, acting as healers. They may mirror unresolved emotions—such as anxiety or fear—urging their humans to confront and heal.

Reciprocal Growth: Humans, in turn, provide safety, love, and healing to pets who may have endured trauma, neglect, or abandonment. Together, both souls grow.

Signs of a Soul Pet Connection

Immediate Recognition: Many describe feeling as though they've "known" a soul pet from the first meeting.

Telepathic Bond: Pets often seem to understand their human's emotions without words, responding instinctively with comfort.

Perfect Timing: A soul pet may arrive precisely when needed—during grief, illness, or transition.

Mirroring Life Lessons: A fearful rescue dog learning trust may help its human open their heart again.

Lasting Impact and Return: Some believe soul pets reincarnate to reunite with their humans, carrying familiar traits across lifetimes.

Soul Pets vs. Spirit Guides

It is important to distinguish:

Soul Pets are individual animals with whom we share a deep earthly bond.

Animal Spirit Guides are archetypal energies or entities that appear symbolically or spiritually, sometimes through dreams or visions.

Yet the two are not entirely separate—a beloved pet that has passed may continue guiding as a spirit animal, offering wisdom from beyond.

Pets as Teachers of Higher Consciousness

Teachers of Love and Forgiveness

Through unconditional love, pets dismantle our self-doubt and shame. Through forgiveness, they show us how to release resentment. Their way of loving is pure and transformative, pointing us toward divine love itself.

Masters of Mindfulness

Pets ground us in the present moment. Watching a dog delight in a walk or a cat luxuriating in a sunbeam invites us to pause, breathe, and remember that life's richness is always found in the now.

Emotional Healers

Pets are highly attuned to their humans. They sense sadness, anxiety, or joy, often mirroring or soothing those states. In their quiet companionship, they absorb pain, offer comfort, and bring healing energy.

Purpose and Resilience

The responsibility of caring for a pet provides humans with a sense of purpose. In times of loneliness, pets offer connection. In moments of despair, they provide resilience. Their presence is a living anchor.

Animal Angels and Nature

Pets also draw us back into connection with the natural world. Daily walks, playful outdoor moments, and time spent observing them awaken our awareness of rhythms greater than ourselves. They remind us that we are not separate from nature but participants in its sacred cycles.

Some call this shift the "Great Pet Awakening"—a growing recognition that our bond with animals is not merely emotional but spiritual, a portal to communion with the divine woven into creation.

Reflective Summary

Animals have always been more than companions; they are angels in earthly form. From Indigenous spirit guides to Hawaiian 'aumakua, from Egyptian gods to modern soul pets, animals have consistently appeared as protectors, messengers, and teachers.

In their loyalty, they embody faithfulness. In their forgiveness, they model compassion. In their presence, they teach mindfulness. Through soul contracts, they enter our lives not by accident but by divine design, guiding us through healing and growth.

To honor an animal is to honor an angel in disguise. To love a pet is to engage in a sacred partnership that uplifts the soul, expands consciousness, and reminds us that the entire natural world is infused with divine presence.

Meditative Reflections

    1. Animal Guide Visualization: Close your eyes and invite an animal—real, symbolic, or remembered—to

step forward in your imagination. What qualities does it embody? What message might it bring?

2. Soul Pet Connection: Recall your pet (past or present). Ask yourself: What life lesson has this soul come to teach me? How has my growth mirrored theirs?

3. Dream Reflection: Think of any dream in which an animal appeared. Write down what you recall. Reflect on whether it may have been a messenger offering wisdom for your current path.

4. Mindful Presence with a Pet: Spend 10 minutes observing your pet without distraction. Watch how they breathe, move, and interact with their environment. Let their presence pull you into the sacred now.

5. Prayer of Gratitude: Whisper a prayer thanking God for sending animal angels into your life. Acknowledge their love, guidance, and the healing they have offered.

Part II

Beyond the Veil

Chapter 4: Echoes of Eternity
The Invisible Thread of Love

The bond between humans and their pets often feels mysterious, as though woven by threads unseen. Anyone who has ever felt their dog sense sadness before a single tear is shed, or their cat curl onto their lap at the exact moment of need, knows this truth: there is something about the connection that transcends words, logic, and sometimes even physical presence.

This experience has been called many things—intuition, soul connection, energetic resonance—but one of the most compelling metaphors comes from the world of modern physics: **quantum entanglement.**

Though grounded in the abstract world of subatomic particles, entanglement serves as a powerful image for describing the invisible, timeless quality of our relationships with animals. Like entangled particles that remain mysteriously connected regardless of distance, the bond with a beloved pet often feels eternal, echoing across space and time even after their physical absence. These are the echoes of eternity—moments in which love defies separation, grief is transformed into presence, and memory becomes a living vibration that continues to nurture the soul.

Quantum Entanglement as a Metaphor

In physics, quantum entanglement refers to the phenomenon where two or more particles become linked so that the state of one instantaneously influences the state of the other, regardless of distance. Albert Einstein famously called it "spooky action at a distance," a phrase that captures both the strangeness and beauty of the concept.

When used as metaphor for the human–pet bond, entanglement suggests several profound truths:

Intuitive Connection

Just as entangled particles mirror one another, the relationship between pet and human often feels intuitively synchronized. A dog may sense its human's anxiety before a word is spoken. A cat may suddenly appear in the room when its owner is grieving, as though drawn by an invisible signal. These experiences feel uncanny, yet they are deeply real, rooted in a kind of intuitive resonance.

Shared Experience

Entangled particles are inseparable not because of physical proximity, but because of their shared history. Likewise, a pet and human, after years of companionship, carry within them a shared field of memory—a tapestry of walks, play, touch, and presence. This history creates a spiritual echo, so that even after death or separation, the connection remains.

A Bond Beyond Presence

Perhaps the most comforting aspect of this metaphor is its reassurance that love persists beyond physical boundaries. Many people feel their pet's presence long after loss, hearing echoes in dreams, sensing them in moments of silence, or feeling them near in times of distress. Just as entangled particles remain linked across distance, the love between pet and human defies absence.

The Human–Pet Bond from Science

While the metaphor of entanglement is poetic, modern science also validates the profound depth of human–animal bonds.

The "Love Hormone"

Research shows that mutual gaze between a dog and its

owner can trigger the release of oxytocin, often called the "love hormone." This biochemical cascade strengthens trust, bonding, and emotional warmth, mirroring the chemical responses between parent and child.

Stress Relief and Mental Health

Pet interactions lower cortisol (the stress hormone) while elevating serotonin and dopamine, neurotransmitters associated with joy and well-being. This explains why time with pets often feels like an oasis of peace amid chaos.

Attachment Theory

From a psychological perspective, pets can function as attachment figures—sources of comfort, safety, and stability. Much like a child's bond with a caregiver, the pet–human bond becomes a secure emotional foundation.

Evolutionary Cooperation

The depth of the bond also reflects evolution. Dogs, for example, co-evolved with humans over tens of thousands of years, developing unique communication skills (like reading facial expressions) that foster intimacy. In this sense, the love we feel for pets is not only emotional—it is written into our shared biological history.

Energy Fields and Vibrational Signatures

Moving from metaphor and science into spirituality, many traditions describe the human–animal bond in terms of energy fields and vibrational resonance.

Foundational Concepts

Vibrational Signatures: Every being has a unique energetic frequency shaped by thought, emotion, and experience.

Energy Fields (Biofields): Living organisms are surrounded by dynamic fields of subtle energy, known as prana in Ayurveda, qi in Chinese medicine, and "biofield" in complementary medicine.

Electromagnetic Evidence: Scientifically, the heart and brain generate measurable fields that extend several feet beyond the body. These fields carry information that can influence others nearby.

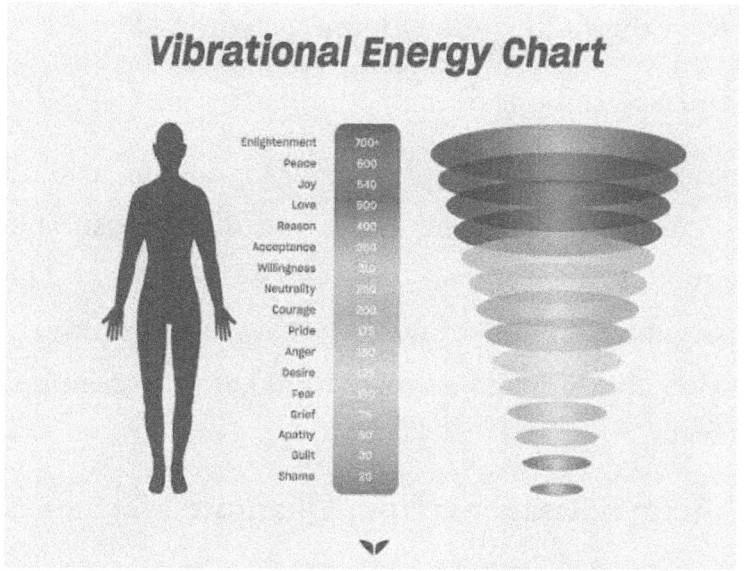

Fig. 1   Vibrational Energy Chart

Connection with Pets

Energy Exchange: Humans and pets continuously exchange energy, responding to one another's moods and emotions.

Resonance: Studies suggest that heart rhythms of humans and pets can synchronize during relaxation, reflecting an energetic harmony.

Intuitive Understanding: Many believe pets perceive these energetic signals instinctively, enabling them to know what their humans feel without words.

Science and Spirit Together

While energy fields in complementary medicine extend beyond current scientific consensus, measurable electromagnetic phenomena provide a bridge. The language of vibration helps describe what many intuitively feel—that pets and humans resonate together in unseen but powerful ways.

Love as Energy: Metaphors from Quantum Mechanics

Beyond entanglement, other quantum principles have been used as metaphors for love.

Superposition: Just as particles exist in multiple states until observed, love can hold many emotions—joy, doubt, longing—at once. It is fluid, evolving, and multifaceted.

Conservation of Energy: In physics, energy cannot be destroyed, only transformed. Similarly, love may shift form—changing from physical companionship to memory, from grief to gratitude—but it never truly disappears.

Physicists caution that these are metaphors, not mechanisms. But for the heart, metaphor can be as meaningful as fact. Quantum imagery allows us to articulate what is otherwise unspeakable: that love, once awakened, reverberates forever.

Echoes After Loss

Perhaps nowhere is the metaphor of entanglement more comforting than in grief. The death of a beloved pet feels like the severing of a lifeline. Yet many people report experiences of continued presence—dreams, sensations, or sudden memories arriving like whispers from beyond.

These are the echoes of eternity—the ongoing resonance of love that death cannot silence. The wag of a tail remembered, the sound of paws on a floor, the imagined warmth of a body still felt on the bed—these are not hallucinations. They are energetic imprints, carried in the heart's field, reverberating like entangled echoes.

Reflective Summary

The bond between humans and pets is at once poetic, scientific, and spiritual. Quantum entanglement offers a metaphor for the invisible, enduring connection that binds souls together beyond distance and death. Science explains how oxytocin, cortisol, and evolutionary history root this bond in biology. Energy fields and vibrational resonance extend the vision, suggesting that our pets literally resonate with us in ways we may not yet fully understand.

Together, these perspectives affirm a central truth: love is never wasted. The love shared with a pet continues to echo, transforming but never vanishing. It is written in memory, imprinted in energy, and alive in spirit.

These echoes of eternity are more than comfort; they are reminders that in the deepest sense, we are never alone.

Meditative Reflections

1. Entanglement Meditation: Close your eyes and imagine a thread of light connecting you and your pet—whether living or passed on. See how this light glows, unbroken across time and space. Rest in its presence.

2. Energy Resonance Practice: Place your hand on your heart, then rest it on your pet (or imagine doing so). Breathe slowly and notice how your rhythms synchronize. Feel the shared resonance.

3. Love Transformation Reflection: Recall a moment of grief after loss. Now ask: how has that love transformed? Has it become memory, gratitude, or guidance? Honor its new form.

4. Mindful Connection: Spend five minutes in stillness with your pet, simply observing them without

distraction. Notice the subtleties of their breath, gaze, and movements. Allow yourself to be drawn into the present moment.

5. Echoes Journal Prompt: Write down one way your pet's presence continues to echo in your life today. Let this reflection remind you that love is energy—it never dies, only changes form.

Chapter 5: The Continuum of Life

The Great Circle of Being

Life does not move in straight lines but in circles. Birth leads to death, death folds back into spirit, and spirit returns once more to life. This is the great rhythm, the eternal continuum that binds every soul—human, animal, plant, and unseen presence—into a shared cosmic journey. The love we feel for our pets, the grief we experience when they depart, and the quiet hope we hold of reunion all find their place within this continuum.

The Continuum of Life is a mystical framework that affirms the interconnection of all existence. Within it, the soul of an animal is not a fleeting spark extinguished by death, but an enduring flame, carried forward into new forms, new lessons, and new expressions of love. Pets, therefore, are not temporary companions but eternal travelers, walking with us across lifetimes in patterns of recognition, healing, and transformation.

Mystical Beliefs About the Animal Afterlife

The Soul's Journey and Reincarnation

Many mystical traditions affirm that animals, like humans, are on a soul journey. Death is not an end but a passage into a subtler realm, where the soul rests before continuing its evolution. An animal's essence—its "soul spirit"—is seen as eternal, unfolding across lifetimes.

Returning in New Forms

It is said that beloved pets may reincarnate, returning to familiar owners or soul groups. Sometimes they come back in the same species; other times they take on new forms. A soul may choose to return as a different kind of animal—or, in some mystical systems, even as a human—to pursue growth and balance.

Interspecies Reincarnation and Soul Fusion

The continuum allows for transformation across species. A cat's soul may one day inhabit a dog, or a bird may become human, if that is the natural arc of its growth. In some traditions, the soul of a departed pet may also blend with the spirit of a new animal, creating a unique fusion of energies—a living bridge between old and new.

After-Death Communication

Countless testimonies describe after-death communications (ADCs) from pets: the rustle of paws on a familiar floor, a sudden warmth on the bed where they once slept, the faint sound of a bark or purr in the night. These experiences bring comfort, affirming that love does not dissolve with death.

End-of-Life and Near-Death Experiences

Stories abound of dying individuals sensing the presence of departed pets, or even being greeted by them in near-death experiences. Such accounts suggest that pets may act as escorts across the threshold, guardians of comfort in our most vulnerable transition.

Soul Purpose and Destiny

Not every animal soul reincarnates. Some choose to remain in the spiritual realm, their purpose fulfilled. There, they exist in peace—free from illness, pain, and earthly struggle—watching over their human companions with quiet love.

Indigenous Teachings

Many Indigenous traditions are rooted in animism, the belief that all things—animals, plants, rivers, mountains—possess a living spirit.

Cycles of Transformation

Some North American tribes believed that souls continue as animals after death, either as continuation or punishment. For example, among the Yurok and Wintūn, the wicked might be reborn as weaker animals or fearsome predators.

Animals as Spirit Guides

Animals are viewed as spirit guides, protectors, and intermediaries who accompany humans throughout life and beyond. Their spirits are honored in ritual, dream, and storytelling, affirming their eternal role in the cosmic web.

The Bridge to Paradise

An ancient legend tells of a bridge to paradise where every animal a person encountered in life awaits them. These animals judge the human's worthiness based on how they were treated. For those who lived with kindness, the animals allow safe passage. For those who caused harm, the animals may block the way. This myth highlights the moral weight of our relationships with animals and the eternal consequences of love—or cruelty.

Eastern Teachings

Eastern traditions often describe life as samsara, an endless cycle of birth, death, and rebirth in which both humans and animals participate.

Hinduism

Animals possess an atman (soul) shaped by karma. A dog may reincarnate as a human if bonded deeply with one, or a human may return as an animal to learn humility. Certain animals, such as cows, are revered as sacred gateways of spiritual evolution.

Buddhism

Animals are sentient beings bound by karma. Rebirth as an animal is often associated with suffering, yet even in this form, the potential for enlightenment remains. Some texts describe animals attaining Buddhahood, while Pure Land interpretations allow humans to transfer merit to beloved pets, enabling their rebirth into paradise.

Jainism

Jainism's doctrine of ahimsa (non-violence) proclaims the equality of all souls. Humans and animals are fellow travelers in samsara, destined for liberation through compassion and non-harm.

Sikhism and Taoism

Sikhism affirms that all beings contain a divine spark and may reincarnate across forms according to karma. Taoism emphasizes harmony with the Tao—the natural order—suggesting that animal souls, like human ones, can cultivate immortality through balance.

Western Teachings

The West offers diverse and often conflicting perspectives on animal afterlife.

Christianity

The Bible is ambiguous about animals in eternity. Some passages (Isaiah 11, Romans 8) envision a redeemed creation where animals share in restoration. Thinkers like Augustine denied animal souls, while modern voices like C.S. Lewis and Billy Graham affirmed hope of their presence in heaven.

Judaism

Rabbinic texts often deny animals an afterlife, but mystical and Hasidic interpretations allow for animal souls, sometimes as vessels of human repentance.

Islam

Animals are recognized as worshippers of God, subject to judgment. Some interpretations suggest their souls return to dust; others believe God may mercifully reunite pets with loving owners in paradise.

Esoteric Traditions

Theosophy: Proposes that animals belong to group souls, gradually evolving toward individuation and potential human incarnation.

Spiritualism: Teaches that all animals continue beyond death and can communicate with humans from the spirit world.

Soul Families and Reincarnating Pets

Soul Families

In mystical teachings, both humans and animals belong to soul families—groups of souls who incarnate together across lifetimes for mutual learning and love. Pets, therefore, are not random companions but chosen members of these families.

Soul Contracts

Before birth, agreements may be made between souls. A dog may agree to teach loyalty. A cat may come to model independence. A parrot may incarnate to awaken joy. These contracts are sacred bonds, designed for growth.

Soul Pets

Some animals are not just companions but soul pets—those with whom we share an unusually deep, transformative bond. Their love reshapes us, teaching lessons that endure long after death.

Returning in a New Body

Mystics affirm that pets may reincarnate to rejoin their humans. Though their appearance may differ, their energy, quirks, or even responses to old nicknames reveal continuity. Many describe a sense of instant recognition upon meeting such a pet.

Reuniting in Spirit

Even if a pet does not reincarnate, traditions hold that all beloved animals will reunite with their humans in the spiritual realm. There, every bond is restored, every love fulfilled, every companion waiting.

The Purpose of the Continuum

The continuum of life is not random—it is purposeful. Pets serve as healers, teachers, and mirrors, helping

humans grow in compassion, forgiveness, and love. Humans, in turn, provide shelter, care, and love that help animals heal from trauma and evolve spiritually. Together, both participate in a sacred exchange, moving step by step toward wholeness.

Reflective Summary

The Continuum of Life affirms that no bond is wasted, no love is lost, and no soul forgotten. Across Indigenous, Eastern, and Western traditions, the testimony is clear: animals, like humans, are eternal beings. They reincarnate, guide, heal, and remain present in spirit long after their physical departure.

The mystical idea of soul families assures us that pets are not accidents in our lives but chosen companions, written into our story by divine design. Whether through reincarnation, afterlife reunion, or eternal presence, their companionship echoes beyond time.

To see life as a continuum is to rest in hope: the love we share with our pets will never fade. It continues across lifetimes, transforms across dimensions, and awaits us in eternity.

Meditative Reflections

1. Circle of Life Visualization: Imagine a glowing circle representing the continuum of life. Place your pet's soul within it, alongside your own. See the circle turning endlessly, carrying both of you together through lifetimes.

2. Soul Family Meditation: Reflect on all the pets you have ever loved. See them gathered as a family of souls, surrounding you with their love. Whisper your gratitude to each.

3. Reincarnation Reflection: Ask yourself: Have I ever felt an instant recognition with an animal? Might this be a soul returning? Write about the possibility.

4. Bridge of Animals Contemplation: Picture crossing a shining bridge after death, with every animal you've ever known waiting to greet you. How does this image shape the way you live now?

5. Gratitude Prayer: Offer a prayer of thanks to God for weaving animals into the continuum of life. Affirm that love is never lost—it simply changes form.

Chapter 6: Signs from Spirit Companions
When Love Learns a New Language

Grief changes the way we listen. After a beloved companion crosses the threshold of this life, the heart strains toward subtler registers—moments that feel uncanny, jolts of knowing, dreams so vivid they linger for days. Many mystical and spiritual teachings suggest these are not accidents of an overburdened imagination but communications—gentle transmissions from our Spirit Companions, the loved ones (including pets) who continue to love us from the other side of the veil.

These transmissions seldom arrive like thunderclaps. More often they are the tender tap on a window, the sudden warmth at the foot of the bed, a collar-jingle no one else hears, the cardinal on the railing exactly on the anniversary morning, the distinct feeling, I am not alone. In the alphabet of the unseen, dreams, visitations, synchronicities, and intuitive "clairs" become the letters love uses to write its messages. Learning to recognize them is not superstition; it is apprenticeship in a deeper attentiveness—the same attentive love our animals modeled for us in life.

This chapter is not an argument for belief; it is a field guide to noticing. It offers a language and a practice so that, when your Spirit Companion speaks, your heart has somewhere to place the meaning.

Dreams and Visitations: When the Night Opens a Door

Visitation Dreams

Not all dreams are equal. Many grievers describe a category that feels qualitatively different: visitation dreams—exceptionally vivid, unusually peaceful, often lucid. In them, the departed appears healthy and luminous, radiating reassurance. The message is simple, nearly universal: I'm okay. I'm with you. Keep going. You wake not disoriented but calmed, as if someone has smoothed the creases of your soul.

Markers of a visitation dream often include:

Hyper-reality: Colors, textures, and emotions feel truer than waking life.

Clarity of message: Words may be few, but meaning is unmistakable.

Afterglow: Peace lingers for hours or days; anxiety lifts; grief softens.

Telepathic Communication

In these dreams, speech is frequently unnecessary. You may receive understanding directly—an inner "click" rather than spoken dialogue. The animal you loved looks into you, and meaning arrives whole—comfort, forgiveness, encouragement—like a chord instead of single notes.

Physical Sensations

Some dreamers report palpable sensation: the press of a small body against the knees, the familiar weight at the foot of the bed, a warm breath at the wrist, the faint rasp of a tongue. Whether understood as memory echo, somatic comfort, or spiritual touch, the balm is real: the nervous system relaxes; the heart steadies.

Practice—Inviting a Visitation Dream

Before sleep, speak to your companion with gratitude. Place a photo or collar by your bedside. Ask for what you need—peace, a sign, a sense of their wellbeing. Promise that you will accept whatever form the answer takes.

Synchronicities and Symbolic Messages: When Meaning Winks

Synchronicities are those meaningful "coincidences" that cluster around loss and love, too precise to feel random. The world seems to align small details into a message delivered at the exact right moment.

Familiar Scents and Sounds

A sudden trace of their scent—that particular sun-warmed fur, a favorite flower, a faint whiff of the shampoo used for bath day—or the soft jingle of a collar from the next room, the click of phantom paws, the thump-thump of a remembered tail: such moments can halt us mid-breath. No one else may notice, but you do, and your body knows—this is them.

Animal Messengers

Nature often acts as courier. A butterfly that insists on circling you, a dragonfly hovering in improbable companionship, a cardinal landing close and singing longer than seems plausible—these arrivals frequently coincide with dates, memories, or decisions. It is as if the world borrows another creature's wings to say, I'm near.

Numbers, Lights, and Little Gifts

Repeating numbers—birthdays, adoption dates, "11:11," "3:33"—may begin appearing on clocks, receipts, or street numbers precisely when you're thinking of them.

Electrical play—flickering lights, a radio that powers on to "your" song—has long been reported during peaks of grief or remembrance.

Unexpected findings—a coin, a feather, a heart-shaped leaf—placed conspicuously on your path can feel like love's breadcrumb trail.

Practice—A Morning of Noticing

Set an intention upon waking: I'm open to kind signs today. Carry a small notebook or open a phone note. Record anything unusual, especially if it links personally to your companion. Review at night; patterns often emerge only in retrospect.

Is It a Sign or a Coincidence? Learning the Texture of Meaning

Skepticism is not a lack of faith; it's a guardian of clarity. You don't honor your companion by believing everything—you honor them by discerning well.

Four touchstones of a genuine sign:

1. **Repetition:** It returns—sometimes thrice in a day, sometimes across a week—more often than chance would predict.

2. **Personal Connection:** It carries your private code—an inside joke, a ritual, a specific toy, a habit only you shared.

3. **Felt Sense:** It arrives with peace or rightness—a full-body yes, not a nervous scramble.

4. **Timeliness:** It coincides with moments that matter—anniversaries, decisions, prayer, spikes of grief.

If it leaves you anxious, threatened, or compulsively checking signs like an oracle, pause. True communications from love stabilize; they do not spin you out. When in doubt, ask inwardly: Does this message make me kinder, calmer, more courageous? If yes, receive it. If no, release it.

How Spirit Companions Speak: Intuition and the "Clairs"

Intuition is the instrument; love is the music. Many people discover that, in grief, their intuitive channels sharpen.

Clairvoyance (clear seeing): Inner images—your pet romping in a field, a flash of their favorite spot—arrive spontaneously, often when you're calm or in nature.

Clairaudience (clear hearing): You "hear" their bark, meow, whistle, or a loving phrase in your mind's

ear with the ring of not me, but given to me.

Clairsentience (clear feeling): A wash of their familiar emotion—playful mischief, serene contentment—moves through your body. Sometimes there's a physical nudge, the brush at your calf, the bed-dip of arrival.

Clair-cognizance (clear knowing): Sudden certainty—don't take that road today; I'm okay; choose rest—drops in whole and unforced.

Practice—Three-Minute Drop-In

Sit, place a hand over your heart. Say your companion's name. Ask one simple question. Breathe for ten slow counts. Notice the first image, word, or feeling that arises. Don't edit. Write it down. Meaning accumulates over days.

Physical and Sensory Signs: The Body Remembers

The body stores a map of companionship—where paws once circled, where a chin rested, how the weight settled at your feet. After death, this map can light up again, briefly.

Presence: The unmistakable sense that someone just entered the room. You turn—no one is there—and yet you're suddenly calm.

Touch: The brush at the ankle, the pressure at the foot of the bed, the gentle warmth on your lap as you read.

Soundscapes: The soft scratch at a closed door, the familiar sigh, a phantom drink from the water bowl.

Object Movement: A favorite toy relocated, a collar placed conspicuously where you'll find it, a photo frame angled toward your chair.

You needn't prove these moments. They are love's small sacraments; receive them and say thank you.

Synchronicities and Soul Families: When Patterns Point to Return

For some, signs cluster not merely as reassurance but as direction—nudging toward a new companion, or hinting at the possibility of a returning soul within a "soul family."

A new animal appears right on time—when you whispered, If I'm meant to love again, open a door.

The newcomer displays eerily familiar quirks: the same nap position, response to an old nickname, a peculiar game you never taught.

You feel the instant knowing—not that bodies are identical, but that energy is.

Whether you hold literal reincarnation or a more poetic "continuity of love," these patterns can be received as blessing: love finding yet another way to be near.

How to Develop and Trust Your Intuition

1) Quiet the Mind, Befriend the Body

Create stillness: A daily five-minute pause conditions your awareness to subtler signals.

Mindfulness & breath: Slow exhale lengthens the body's safety signal; safety heightens perception.

Somatic cues: Learn your tells—heart warmth, belly ease, shoulders lowering—these often accompany genuine guidance.

Nature time: The more time among trees, water, and sky, the cleaner the inner signal. Noise recedes, nuance returns.

2) Engage the Process

Journal: Date entries. Record dreams, signs, nudges. Clarity accrues in patterns.

Ask & intend: "Please show me a kind, unmistakable sign today." Then let go. Grasping clogs the channel; gratitude clears it.

Create: Sketch, hum, write—creativity bypasses the gatekeeping mind and gives spirit a canvas.

3) Recognize and Act

Feel the tone: True guidance carries calm authority, not urgency or fear.

First thought best thought: The first, clean impulse often precedes analysis.

Low-stakes practice: Build trust choosing small things by feel—route, tea, timing—then note results. Confidence grows.

4) Gentle Safeguards

Healthy discrimination: If "messages" increase anxiety, step back. Seek grounding, counsel, rest.

Compassion for yourself: Grief heightens sensitivity; that's tenderness, not weakness.

Integration over obsession: Signs are seasoning, not the meal. Live, love, practice, and let signs be gifts, not requirements.

Rituals that Welcome Communication

Ritual makes space for meaning to gather. Consider these simple, beautiful practices:

The Companion Corner: A small altar with photo, collar, favorite toy, a candle. Sit there when you wish to speak or listen.

Anniversary Light: On birthdays, adoption days, or crossing days, light a candle and tell a favorite story aloud. Invite a sign if one wishes to come.

The Walk We Still Share: Take a weekly walk you used to enjoy together. Speak as you go. Notice nature's responses.

The Gratitude Letter: Write letters to your companion—what you miss, what you learned, what you promise to carry forward. Place them beneath the candle or bury them beneath a tree.

Practice—Closing the Day

Each night, name three ways love touched you—dream, memory, sign, kindness from a stranger. "More, please, and thank you." Then sleep with the window of the heart slightly open.

Stories from the Threshold (Composite Vignettes)

The Collar's Song: After Mateo's terrier, Nala, passed, he removed her collar and placed it in a drawer. Three mornings later, as he considered canceling a difficult conversation, he heard the collar jingle clearly from the empty hallway. He kept the appointment. The call brought reconciliation. He wrote in his journal, Nala says: be brave.

Red Wing on the Railing: On the first spring without her cat, Noor asked for a sign. A red-winged blackbird landed on her railing, sang for two full minutes, and returned at the same hour for three days. The fourth day, Noor signed adoption papers for a shy shelter cat with a tiny flame-shaped mark on his chest. She named him Ember.

The Dream of the Meadow: Jordan dreamed of his German Shepherd running in a vast meadow. No limp, no pain. The dog stopped, looked back with bright eyes, and Jordan "heard," I am light now. He woke radiant. The meadow became his meditation image; anxiety, once constant, eased.

These vignettes are not proofs—they are pearls. String enough together and you find a necklace sturdy enough to wear through your days.

Living With the Signs: Integration and Ethics

Signs are for you, not to be wielded at others. Hold them with humility. Resist comparing stories or grading your experience against someone else's. What arrives for you is tailored to your path, your language of love.

When signs encourage kindness, courage, patience, and trust, they harmonize with every sacred tradition's best wisdom. When they urge harm, panic, or grandiosity, they are not your Spirit Companion. Close the door; open a window; breathe; ask again for what is good, true, and beautiful.

Reflective Summary

Spirit Companions—the loved ones and pets who have crossed—often speak in the dialects of tenderness: vivid dreams, felt presences, gentle sounds, timely birds, repeating numbers, little gifts on the path, and, most of all, the inner yes that accompanies them. True signs carry four signatures: repetition, personal meaning, peaceful felt sense, and timeliness. They do not demand; they reassure. They do not confuse; they clarify.

Learning this language is less about acquiring a new belief than about refining attention. We quiet the mind, befriend the body, journal patterns, ask sincerely, and release control. We practice small acts of trust. We hold ritual spaces where love can gather. And we receive what comes without clutching.

In the end, signs matter not because they prove an afterlife, but because they let love keep doing its work:

healing, guiding, steadying, and expanding us. Your companion's message is the same one they lived beside you: I am with you. Keep loving. Keep going. When we let that message shape our days, we discover that the boundary between worlds is thinner than a breath—and love is the bridge.

Meditative Reflections

    1.   Open-Window of the Heart (5 minutes)

Sit quietly. Imagine a small window at the center of your chest. On the inhale, the window opens; on the exhale, soft light flows out. Say your companion's name once. Whisper: I'm listening. Notice any image, word, or sensation that arrives. Receive without judging.

    2.   Feather, Coin, Leaf

During a walk, ask for a simple token if one is kind to offer. If a coin, feather, or heart-shaped leaf appears conspicuously, pause. Place a hand to your heart and say, Thank you. If nothing appears, say, thank you for loving me anyway. Gratitude keeps the channel clear.

    3.   Visitation Invitation (bedside ritual)

Place a photo or collar by a candle. Speak three memories that make you smile. Ask for a peaceful dream if it serves the highest good. Promise you will accept rest as an answer too. Upon waking, write one sentence about how you feel—no analysis, just tone.

4. The Calm Test

When a potential sign appears, ask: Does this make me calmer, kinder, more courageous? If yes, integrate: take the call, make the apology, choose the walk. Let signs shape behavior; meaning ripens in action.

5. The Gratitude Letter

Write a letter beginning, Beloved friend, here is what you taught me... Read it aloud at your Companion Corner. Burn or keep it. Either way, end with: Our love continues in new forms. I will carry your lesson today.

Part III

Walking Through Grief

Chapter 7: The Human Heart and the Void – When Love Leaves Footprints in Silence

There is a particular quiet that follows the death of a beloved companion animal. It is not the ordinary quiet of an empty room but an ache that expands to fill the hallways, a silence made of missing rhythms—the collar that no longer jingles, the water bowl that stays full, the walk you do not take. This silence is not emptiness; it is absence shaped like love. Within it, the human heart must learn to breathe again.

Some wonder why the grief for a pet can feel as searing—or more so—than the grief for a human relative. The answer is simple and profound: the bond with a pet is often pure, constant, and uncomplicated. It is forged in daily rituals and wordless devotion, in quiet mornings and faithful nights. In the economy of the soul, such bonds hold tremendous weight. When they break, the heart experiences not a small bruise but a tectonic shift.

This chapter explores the unique shape of pet loss, why it can feel disenfranchised and isolating, how it affects the brain and body, and what compassionate practices help us cross the landscape of absence. It is both map and companion—because the road is real, and you do not have to walk it alone.

The Human–Animal Bond: Why This Hurts So Much

Uncomplicated Connection

Human relationships, beautiful as they are, can be dense with history, expectation, and unresolved complexity. With a pet, the channel is often clear. Their presence says, You are enough. I'm here. When a bond has been primarily affirming and stable, its interruption can feel like losing oxygen—especially for those who rarely receive such unconditional mirroring elsewhere.

Constant Companionship

Pets live in the borderlands of our days: before the coffee, after the meeting, during the long watch of midnight. They pad through the mundane and the

momentous alike. When they die, the house itself seems bereaved. Familiar routes turn strange; chairs look too big; evenings lengthen. The nervous system has lost a regulatory rhythm, and the body protests.

Source of Purpose

Feeding, walking, grooming, training, playing—these are not chores; they are bonding rituals. They give structure to time and meaning to motion. The death of a pet removes a lattice of purpose. The calendar loosens, and with it the sense of one's role: If I am not their person now, who am I?

Unconditional Love

Pets love without agenda. They do not measure our worth by salary, status, or flawlessness. Their gaze confers belonging. The loss of that gaze can feel like a spiritual amputation. For the estranged, the isolated, the overburdened caregiver, the pet may have functioned as primary attachment figure—the safe base. Losing a safe base is destabilizing at the deepest level.

The Void of Disenfranchised Grief

Grief Without a Public

Disenfranchised grief is loss that society does not fully recognize or support. Pet bereavement often falls here. Few employers offer leave; few communities host public rituals. Friends mean well and wound anyway—You can get another dog. The message received: your sorrow is excessive. So, the grieving becomes quiet, and loneliness compounds the pain.

Shame and Comparison

Some feel guilty that losing a pet hurts more than previous human losses. But grief is not a contest; it is attachment in motion. The intensity of sorrow mirrors the quality of the bond, the frequency of daily contact, and the degree of emotional reliance. The love was real. Therefore the grief is real.

The Cost of Stifled Mourning

Grief is an internal response; mourning is its outward expression—telling stories, crying with others, participating in ritual. When mourning is blocked, grief can stagnate into complicated grief, anxiety, or depression. The remedy is not to "be strong," but to be accompanied.

How Loss Lands in the Body and Brain

Neurochemistry of Bond and Break

Shared gaze and touch elevate oxytocin, the bonding hormone; routine and play calibrate dopamine and serotonin. When a pet dies, the brain experiences a withdrawal of soothing inputs while stress hormones like cortisol rise. This is why grief can feel like panic, fog, or exhaustion. You are not "overreacting." Your body is accurately registering separation distress.

Disrupted Routines, Disoriented Self

The nervous system loves predictability. Remove anchor points—morning walks, bedtime cuddles—and the day loses entrainment. Rebuilding a gentle rhythm (even without replacing the pet) helps the brain regain steadiness.

Grief Reactivates Old Pain

Loss is a master key; it can unlock rooms we didn't know we still inhabited. For those with earlier bereavements, attachment wounds, or medical caregiver fatigue, pet loss may resurface prior sorrows asking for completion. This is not regression; it is an invitation to integration.

What Healthy Grieving Looks Like (And doesn't)

There is no single map, but a few trustworthy models help normalize the terrain:

Continuing Bonds: The goal is not to "let go" but to re-form the relationship—from physical presence to inner connection, memory, ritual, and meaning.

Dual-Process Model: We oscillate between loss-oriented coping (crying, remembering, honoring) and restoration-oriented coping (managing tasks, rebuilding routines). Healthy grief swings.

Worden's Four Tasks of Mourning (William Worden, adapted):

1. Acknowledge the reality of the loss.
2. Process the pain of grief.
3. Recalibrate roles and routines without the pet.
4. Reinvest in life while maintaining a lasting inner bond.

If someone demands linear "stages," smile gently. Grief is not a staircase; it is a tide.

Coping With the Emptiness: Practices That Help

1) Acknowledge the Pain

Give yourself explicit permission: This is real. This matters. Tears are intelligent; they complete stress cycles and soften the body for love's return.

2) Create a Memorial

Ritual metabolizes sorrow. Consider: a photo altar with collar and candle; a memory box; a paw-print casting; a small ceremony in a favorite place; a letter of goodbye (or "see you in another form"). Ritual gives grief somewhere to go.

3) Seek the Right Company

Find one friend who "gets it," or join a pet loss support group (many exist online). Share stories. Listen to others. Human nervous systems co-regulate; companionship is medicine.

4) Allow Time to Heal

Grief has its own clock. Resist the two extremes—replacing immediately to stop feeling or delaying forever out of fear of disloyalty. A new pet, when the time is right, is not a replacement; it is a new relationship.

5) Volunteer When Ready

Serving at a shelter, fostering, or donating in your pet's name can transmute pain into purpose. It's not distraction; it's alchemy.

The Guilt That Comes with Love (Euthanasia, What-Ifs, and the Loop)

Few decisions are as heavy as consenting to euthanasia—or as common in companion-animal care. Guilt plays predictable games:

Hindsight Bias: I should have known earlier.

Magical Responsibility: If I had tried one more treatment…

False Logic: Because I decided the time, I caused the death.

Reframe with compassion:

You ended suffering; you did not end love.

You chose mercy with the information and resources you had.

Your companion did not measure your love by days added, but by comfort offered.

Write a letter to your pet about this decision. Let them "reply" from their wisdom: Thank you for the gentle path.

When the House Isn't the Only One Grieving (Children, Elders, and Other Pets)

Children

Offer clear, age-appropriate truth (avoid "went to sleep"). Invite questions repeatedly; grief for kids is recycled at each new developmental stage. Create a shared ritual: draw pictures, read a story, plant a flower. Let them see you cry; it teaches that tears and love coexist.

Elders

For older adults, a pet may be lifeline and daily structure. Watch for functional declines after loss. Gentle check-ins, shared meals, and help with small memorials can prevent silent spirals.

Surviving Pets

Animals grieve too: changes in appetite, pacing, clinginess, searching behavior. Maintain routine, increase gentle play and contact, and consider bringing them to say goodbye (if appropriate). Offer your regulated presence; they read your nervous system.

Rebuilding a Life That Still Knows How to Love

Self-Care Is Not Cosmetic

Eat warm food, drink water, touch earth, sleep more. Grief is metabolically expensive. Treat your body like someone you're responsible for caring for—because you are.

A New Routine (Without Pretending)

Create bookends to your day: a morning breath and blessing; an evening candle and three gratitude. Routines are scaffolding while the heart heals.

Meaning-Making

Ask: What did this companion teach me? How do I live that lesson now? Perhaps it is radical presence, unembarrassed affection, or daily play. Let their legacy shape your living.

Considering a New Companion

When the inner terror of forgetting softens into the desire to love again, you are not betraying; you are continuing the river of care that your pet helped carve through your life. Go slow. Listen deeply. The right connection won't erase; it will harmonize.

Gentle Tools for Hard Days

The Empty-Bowl Ritual: Place the bowl on the altar. Add a fresh flower weekly. Whisper thanks for nourishment shared.

The Walk You Still Take: Walk your old route once a week. Speak memories aloud. Notice what nature returns.

The Story Hour: Invite a friend to listen while you tell three favorite stories. Laughter is allowed; it is a cousin of love.

The Date of the Heart (anniversaries): Plan something kind on purpose: visit a favorite park, cook the treat you never shared, write a one-page letter titled "What You Taught Me This Year."

What to Say When Others Don't Understand (Scripts)

To dismissive remarks: "I know it might seem small from the outside, but this was family to me."

To your employer: "I'm grieving a significant loss and would benefit from a day to handle personal matters and memorial arrangements."

To yourself (when the spiral starts): "Pain is proof of love. I can let this wave pass and still choose what's kind next."

If Grief Keeps Getting Heavier (When to Seek Extra Support)

Reach for professional support if you notice persistent inability to function, intrusive guilt, self-harm thoughts, or isolation that deepens over weeks. A grief-informed therapist (many specialize in pet loss) provides structured accompaniment through the hardest stretches.

Reflective Summary

Pet loss is not a small grief; it is a fundamental reorganization of attachment. The human–animal bond is unique—steady, uncomplicated, daily—and its rupture reverberates through body, brain, routine, and identity. Society often minimizes this pain, creating a disenfranchised grief that isolates precisely when companionship is most needed.

Healing does not mean forgetting, replacing, or "moving on." Healthy mourning means continuing bonds—allowing the relationship to evolve from physical presence to inner presence, from rituals of care to rituals of remembrance, from shared routines to embodied legacy. We rebuild rhythm, gather support, honor guilt with truth and compassion, include children and surviving pets in our rituals, and let meaning slowly crystallize around what the love taught us.

In time, the void becomes a vessel—not empty, but spacious enough to hold sorrow and gratitude, memory and new beginnings. The silence changes quality. It is no longer the sound of loss alone but the resonance of a love that has learned another way to stay.

Meditative Reflections

    1.   Hand on Bowl, Hand on Heart (4 minutes)

Place one hand over your heart, one on your pet's empty bowl (or another keepsake). Inhale: Thank you. Exhale: I release you from suffering. Repeat slowly for five breaths. Whisper one lesson they taught you; promise one way you'll live it this week.

    2.   The Chair of Presence (5–10 minutes)

Sit where your companion loved to rest. Close your eyes. Sense the outline of their weight, the warmth they left. Say, "You are part of my story. I carry you." Allow a memory to rise; let your face soften into a smile or tears without judgment.

3. Three-Lantern Ritual (evening)

Light three candles (or imagine them):

Lantern of Gratitude—name one gift they gave.

Lantern of Permission—name one feeling you allow tonight.

Lantern of Continuance—name one small act of kindness you'll offer tomorrow in their honor.

4. Walking the Missing (a weekly practice)

Walk a route you once shared. At each corner, pause and breathe. At the end, place your palm on your chest and say, "Where you are, love is." Notice any sign or kindness encountered; write it down when you return.

5. Letter of Mercy (any time guilt returns)

Write: Dear [Name], I am sorry for… Then switch hands or perspective and write their reply beginning, Beloved, thank you for… Read both aloud. Seal the exchange with a hand on your heart and a long exhale.

Chapter 8: Healing in Silence and Expression
The White Coat and the Cracked Heart

The clinical day begins with a checklist: labs, rounds, consults, procedures, charts. The heart, however, keeps its own list: the collar still on the hook, the empty bed at home, the reflex to save a bite of breakfast for a friend who will not come. For physicians and veterinarians, grief often runs beneath the surface like an underground river—audible only where it meets the light.

Medicine prizes steadiness. We cultivate the neutral face, the measured tone, the steady hand. These are good gifts to patients and families; they are also, in grief, a double-edged blade. The physician's dilemma is not whether to be composed—that matters—but how to remain human without splintering, and how to let sorrow move without flooding. This chapter is a field guide for that delicate balance: the art of healing in silence and expression.

The Challenge: Compartmentalizing Grief in Professional Life

Stoicism as a Skill—and a Risk

From the first days of training, clinicians learn to manage emotion so we can act. We deliver bad news with clarity. We hold the line in crisis. We witness pain, remain, and work. This practiced composure is a clinical skill—but when a beloved pet dies, the same habit can become a corset: it holds us upright while making it hard to breathe.

Two Selves, One Body

There is no neat border between "doctor" and "pet parent." The person who pronounces time of death at noon is the same person who, three hours later, will unlock a door to an empty greeting. Expecting the professional self to erase the personal self breeds inner contradiction and the whisper: What's wrong with me that I can't just get over this? Nothing is wrong.

Attachment is working as designed.

Fear of Seeming Unprofessional

Because pet loss is often disenfranchised grief, many clinicians fear that visible sorrow over an animal will be taken as weakness. We worry our tears will be misunderstood. Yet the truth is simpler: tears are evidence of love, and love is evidence of a life attuned to life. We can choose when and where to express them—not whether they're valid.

The Veterinary crucible

Veterinarians navigate a singular pressure: engaging grief daily while managing euthanasia decisions, compassion fatigue, and client projections—then grieving their own animals amidst it. The expectation to be desensitized is both false and harmful. The goal is not desensitization; it is skillful sensitivity.

What Silence Can—and Cannot—Do

Silence can keep you functioning through a shift. It can protect privacy and professionalism. But unprocessed silence stores sorrow in the body: headaches, tight jaws, shallow breath, sleeplessness, a gray fog. Healing silence feels different: it is chosen, time-bound, and followed by release. The key is oscillation—moving between containment and safe expression so the nervous system learns, I can feel this and still do my work.

Healing in Silence: Inner Practices for Clinicians

1) Name, Don't Numb

A whisper to yourself between rooms: "This is grief."

Neuroscience is clear—labeling emotion lowers its intensity. Add a kind truth: "I can hold this for now; I will tend it later."

2) The Sacred Pause (30–90 seconds)

In a stairwell, call room, or car: feet on floor, one hand on chest, one on abdomen.

> Inhale to a count of 4, exhale to 6 (longer exhale tones the vagus nerve).

> On each exhale say softly: "Let." On each inhale: "Be."

> Three cycles can reset the autonomic tide.

3) Micro-Grounding Between Encounters

> Cold water on wrists.

> Orienting: give your eyes three neutral objects to name (clock, pen, door), then one beautiful thing (tree, sky).

> Physiological sigh: inhale, tiny top-up inhale, long sigh out. Twice.

4) Private Rituals

Keep a small token (tag, ribbon, photo) in a pocket. When touched, it says: I see you, love.

Set a phone reminder at a gentle hour: "Check in. One minute for you." Breathe, feel, return.

5) The Boundaried Journal

Five minutes before bed. Three lines only:

1. What I felt today (one word).

2. One memory of my companion.

3. One mercy I will offer myself tomorrow.

Close the notebook; let it hold the rest.

Healing in Expression: Letting the River Move

1) Speak to the Right Ears

Not all colleagues can hold this. Find the one who can—or a peer group, chaplain, therapist, or veterinary/healthcare support circle. Say what is true without apologizing for its scale. Sorrow shrinks shame when spoken in safety.

2) Professional Support Is Professionalism

If grief disrupts sleep, appetite, focus, or makes the day feel unendurable, that is not failure; that is a signal. A grief-informed clinician or counselor can offer structure, language, and permission.

3) Ritualize Remembrance

Companion Corner at home: photo, collar, candle, a sprig of green.

Anniversary Light: on key dates, tell a favorite story aloud.

Letter Exchange: write to your companion; then write their reply to you from mercy's voice. Read both. Keep or burn.

4) Love in Motion

Volunteer, foster, mentor a trainee through their first loss conversation, donate in your pet's name, plant a tree. Action turns ache into agency without rushing the heart.

The Art of De-Compartmentalization (Without Drowning)

Think rhythm, not rupture. Build small, scheduled portals where emotion is welcomed, so it doesn't burst the dam later.

1) Scheduled Worry / Weeping Time (10–20 minutes)

Set a daily appointment with your grief. When thoughts intrude during work, say: "Not now, dear heart—7:30 is for us." Keep the date. Paradoxically, grief intrudes less when it is guaranteed a place.

2) Transition Routines

Create a threshold ritual between clinic and home:

> At the door: hand on jamb, say, I set down what is not mine; I carry forward what is love.

> Wash hands slowly—name what you release into the water (guilt, over-responsibility), name what you keep (kindness, memory).

3) The Compassion Triangle

When emotion spikes, check three corners:

> Body: what sensation? (tight chest)

Belief: what story? (I should have caught it sooner)

Behavior: what's kind now? (hand to heart, slow breath, message a friend tonight)

Small, repeatable acts re-trust your own steadiness.

Strategies for Balancing Emotion and Composure (Clinician's Playbook)

1. Acknowledge & Label

"This is sadness." "This is guilt." "This is love in pain." Label → regulate.

2. Create Space to Feel

Sacred pauses, journaling, brief walks, prayer/meditation. Schedule them like consults.

3. Intentional Support

Choose your listeners. Consider peer groups, Schwartz-style rounds, or confidential supervision.

4. Honor Through Action

Memorialize, serve, donate, teach. Let meaning loop back into the work you do.

5. Adjust Expectations

Ask for humane scheduling when possible. Communicate with supervisors: "I'm experiencing a personal bereavement; I may need brief decompression between difficult conversations this week." Boundaries protect patients, too.

Euthanasia, Guilt, and the Physician's Tender Logic

End-of-life decisions for animals often entangle mercy with doubt. Three distortions commonly visit clinicians:

Hindsight Bias: believing you should have known sooner.

Control Illusion: assuming one more test or day would have changed fate.

Moral Self-Attack: equating the act of consenting to euthanasia with betrayal.

Reframes that heal:

You did not end love; you ended suffering.

You chose with the information you had, not omniscience.

Your companion measured your love by comfort given, not time extended.

A brief mantra in moments of spiral: "Mercy is not failure. Mercy is fidelity.

The Physiology and Sanctity of Tears

Tears are not the opposite of composure; they are composure completing a cycle.

Emotional tears contain stress chemistry the body is ready to release; crying activates oxytocin and endorphins—nature's self-soothing kit.

Suppressing tears increases sympathetic arousal—heart rate, blood pressure, vigilance. Across time, repression costs the body.

In many traditions, tears are sacrament—salt that carries prayer. For the clinician, tears in the right container (privacy, ritual, trusted company) are medicine.

A brief practice: place a box of tissues beside your Companion Corner. When tears come, let three fall. Whisper, "This is love leaving the body as water so it can return as breath." Then breathe.

Special Notes for Veterinarians and Animal-Facing Clinicians

Secondary Loss: Daily exposure to others' pet loss can re-activate your own. Build micro-debriefs after euthanasia appointments (2–5 minutes).

Moral Distress: When client decisions conflict with your sense of best care, name it as moral distress; consult peers; protect your spirit.

Ritual in Clinic: A small, consistent practice—lighting a tea light at the end of a euthanasia day, a gratitude note wall for animals' names—helps teams metabolize sorrow together.

Team Compassion Culture: Normalize brief check-ins: "Color today?" (green/yellow/red). No analysis, just support.

Restoring Rhythm: Self-Care That Respects Reality

Body: warm meals, water, sunlight to the eyes in the morning, 20 minutes of gentle movement.

Sleep: a wind-down anchor (dim lights, hot shower, phone away), and a grief notebook on the nightstand for the 2 a.m. surge.

Nature: ten minutes outside is nervous-system first aid.

Beauty: music, a poem, a leaf you pocket on rounds—beauty is not luxury; it is counter-inflammation for the soul.

The "New Normal" Is Not Lesser—It's Wiser

You will not be the same clinician after this loss. You will be softer where it matters and

clearer where it counts. Your presence with patients at the threshold will carry a credibility that training cannot confer. This is legacy: your companion's love stitching into your bedside manner, your consent conversations, your silences and your timing.

When (or if) a new animal comes, welcome them as a new relationship, not a replacement. Love is a river with many turns; every bend remembers the whole.

Reflective Summary

Clinicians are taught to hold steady; grief asks us to also let go. The art is not choosing one over the other but learning the oscillation: silence that steadies the hand, expression that softens the heart. Pet loss, often minimized by culture, is major attachment rupture. It reverberates through identity, routine, and physiology. Stoicism may keep the room calm; self-compassion keeps the clinician whole.

Healing comes by rhythm: micro-pauses between patients, scheduled spaces to feel, rituals that honor the bond, the courage to seek support, and the humility to adjust expectations. Tears, far from unprofessional, are sacred physiology—releasing, regulating, and re-consecrating your capacity to love and to serve.

In time, the white coat and the cracked heart reconcile. Composure remains, but not as armor—rather as clarity. And beneath it, a stream of tenderness continues to run, irrigating the desert places of your day. This is healing in silence and expression: a steady professionalism woven with a living humanity.

Meditative Reflections

1. Stairwell Pause (60–90 seconds)

Stand with feet hip-width.

Inhale 4, exhale 6, three cycles.

Whisper: "I am here. This is grief. I can do the next kind thing."

Enter the next room with your breath, not your fear, in charge.

2. Pocket Token, Pocket Breath

Keep a small token in your pocket. Each time you touch it, take one physiological sigh (inhale + top-up + long exhale). Silently say your companion's name once. Let warmth replace ache for a beat.

3. Evening De-Compartmentalize (7 minutes)

Light a candle at your Companion Corner.

Journal three lines: Feeling | Memory | Mercy.

If tears come, allow them for one song's length. Snuff candle with gratitude.

4. Threshold Ritual (Homecoming)

- At your door: place a hand on the frame.

- Say: "I set down what is not mine. I carry forward what is love."

- Wash hands slowly, releasing the day into the water.

5.   Letter of Mercy (for Euthanasia Guilt)

•   Write: Dear [Name], here is how I tried to love you at the end…

•   Then switch perspective: Beloved, here is how you did love me…

•   Read aloud. Place both letters beneath the candle or bury them in the garden.

6.   Sunday Reset Walk (20 minutes)

Walk a route you once shared. Name three beauties aloud (light on leaves, a child's laughter, warm pavement). At the end, hand to heart: "Mercy is fidelity. Thank you for teaching me."

Chapter 9: Coco's Story
Grief in Those Left Behind
I Am Still Here

My name is Coco. I am the one who stayed.

The day the house grew quiet, I learned that silence has weight. It sits on the couch where we used to curl together; it pools at the threshold where I waited for a key in the door. The water bowl is still, but the air moves differently, as if the house itself is holding its breath. I'm told that those we love "cross over," that love keeps traveling even when paws stop, that bodies rest while bonds continue. I do not understand all those words. I understand absence. I understand your scent when you are sad. I understand the way your shoulders fall when you try to be brave for me.

I am not a philosopher. I live by routine, by warmth, by the sound of your steps. My grief is not an idea—it is behavior, appetite, sleep. You ask what helps a surviving pet. Let me answer as only I can: from the floor, from the window, from beside your chair.

How Grief Feels in My Body

You call them signs. I call them what happens now.

My voice changes. Sometimes I whine or call out to rooms as if sound could summon the one who is missing. If I yowl or bark more, I am not misbehaving; I am locating.

I stick close. I follow you from room to room because the map has changed and you are my last landmark. When I press against you, I am asking, Are we still two? Are we safe?

Food tastes different. Grief dims flavor. I may nibble or refuse a meal. Sit with me. Warm the food. Add a favorite topper. Let my appetite remember pleasure slowly.

Sleep is not sleep. I nap too long in the day and pace at night, trying old beds and new corners. Sometimes I curl in the place that held our friend's scent. It comforts me the way their shirt comforts you.

Habits slip. I know where the door is, and yet I may forget. A clean house is less important than a calm heart. If I have an accident, I am asking for patience, not punishment.

I search. I visit the window where they used to look out with me. I stand at the spot where you used to fill two bowls and stare. I am not confused; I am remembering.

You might notice I groom more, or less. If I am a cat, you may see me work my tongue until a furrow appears—a way to manage a feeling too big for a small body. If I am a dog, you may see my paws grow damp as I lick away the edge of panic. These are not defects; they are coping.

What Helps Me (Said Simply)

Ritual is love shaped into time. When the world has changed, give me anchors.

Hold the routine. Keep mealtimes close to what they were. Walk me at familiar hours. Bedtime is not just sleep; it is safety rehearsed.

Offer gentle extras. A longer cuddle. A slower walk. A new puzzle feeder. For cats, a window perch warmed by sun, a higher shelf to watch the world. For dogs, a sniffari on a new trail—let my nose lead; the mind follows the nose to calmer places.

Let me say goodbye (if you choose). Some of us need to see and sniff the stillness to understand that seeking will not bring a return. Others will take a single breath and turn away. Watch me. Trust what I show you.

Name the house again. "Chair, blanket, backyard, toy box." When you say the names of our places while we walk through them together, my body learns the new map alongside yours.

If I make mistakes—chew, scratch, pace—remember punishment tightens sorrow. Redirection, praise for calm, a safe den or quiet room—these loosen the knot.

How Your Grief Feels to Me

I am fluent in your nervous system. I read your hands, your breath, the quiet between your words. When you try not to cry, I feel the held breath like thunder. Let some tears fall where I can see. They smell like salt and relief. When your voice softens to say my name, the house steadies.

Please do what you must to heal—call a friend who understands, light a candle, make a memory box. When you care for your grief, you are also caring for me. If you can, save a piece of your calm for our time together: our meal, our walk, our game. Your steadiness is the dock I tie my little boat to when waves rise.

Do not hurry to bring another animal home for my sake. I am still learning the new world. New scents can be stress. Wait until both of us can welcome another heartbeat with curiosity instead of fear. When the right time comes, I will tell you with loose shoulders, a bright eye, a ready wag or purr.

When You Should Ask for Help (For Me)

If I stop eating for more than a day, if water goes untouched, if my ribs begin to show—call a veterinarian. My grief sits inside a body; bodies can tip into danger. Cats, especially, can sicken quickly when they do not eat. If anxiety wraps around me until I cannot rest, a veterinary behaviorist may offer training plans, pheromones, or medicine to give my brain a chance to remember calm.

Help is not failure. Help is love that learned a new tool.

What I Know About Your Grief (From the Floor)

You think grief is only tears. I know grief is also pacing, staring, forgetting keys, not tasting tea, remembering the way the afternoon used to sound. Sometimes you are angry at the one who left. Sometimes you are angry at yourself. Sometimes you scold the universe—Too soon. Too hard. I do not judge your words. Let them be wind; I am the anchor at your ankle.

If guilt bites—about decisions at the end, about what you did or didn't do—sit with me and speak aloud as if reporting to a friend: We did our best with what we knew. We chose comfort over clock. We loved with our whole hands. I will press my head into your knees at the exact right line.

When fear comes—What is my life now? Who am I without them? I suggest something simple: go outside together. Stand where air moves. Name three good things we can sense. The world remains, and it is not indifferent to us.

The Family Pack: When Everyone Hurts

I see how the house changes when grief is shared. Children look to adults for the rules of sadness. Let them see a tear on your cheek and a smile when a good story arrives; both truths can live in one face. Invite them to draw our friend, to put a favorite toy in the memory box, to say goodnight to the photo. Do not hide the picture when they laugh at something silly five minutes later. Laughter does not betray love.

If other animals remain, watch us without panic. We may circle each other differently for a while, adopt new stations in the room, or wander together to the door we used to wait at. Keep shared scents—a blanket, a bed—for a little while.

Let us visit and learn, without forcing closeness.

How We Heal Together (A Dog's / Cat's Short List)

Check-ins. Sit on the floor once a day at my level. Let me choose the distance. If I come close, place your hand where I like it best. Stay there three slow breaths longer than usual.

Low lights, slow evenings. After dinner, fewer screens, quieter. Grief is loud, the heart needs low tide.

Small adventures. A new trail, a new toy, a box to explore. Novelty that does not overwhelm reminds the brain that curiosity still fits.

A simple sentence. Whisper to me every night: We're still us. I do not understand grammar; I understand tone. Say it like a promise.

When the House is Ready to Welcome Again

If a new companion comes, we will make room on purpose. Keep a piece of fabric with our old friend's scent in a keepsake box; wash the beds and bowls before the new arrival. Hold two truths at once: no one replaces anyone, and love expands. Introduce in stages—doorway scent swaps, brief greetings, predictable routines. Choose patience over proof. Let the new heartbeat teach us who they are.

I will show you what I need. You will show me what you can give. This is how families keep happening.

Reflective Summary

Grief in the animals who remain is real, embodied, and legible if we listen with our eyes, ears, and hands. We vocalize, cling, withdraw, forget, search, sleep poorly, skip meals. These changes are not disobedience; they are mourning behaviors. What steadies us is not perfection but predictability—routines that remain, affection we can count, and environments that feel safe. Enrichment that engages our senses (sniff walks, vertical spaces, puzzles) helps curiosity loosen sorrow's grip. Patience and gentle redirection beat punishment every time.

Your grief matters to us. When you regulate yourself—cry when you need, breathe slowly when you can, seek support—you regulate us. Delay new adoptions until both nervous systems can welcome novelty. Seek veterinary care if appetite, weight, or anxiety slide into risk; consider behavior support when grief gets stuck. In family systems, model honesty and ritual, and allow different grieving styles to coexist without judgment.

Most of all, remember this: we attend to the present so you can remember the past without drowning in it. The bowl, the leash, the window, the chair—these become altars when we meet them together with tenderness. In time, the silence of the house changes from a hollow to a vessel, holding memory and new laughter side by side. I am still here. We are still us. And love—yours and mine—continues to learn its way forward.

Meditative Reflections

    1.   Floor-Level Check-In (3 minutes)

Sit on the floor at your pet's height. Place one hand on your belly, one on your chest. Breathe in for 4, out for 6. Say your pet's name. Let them approach or simply rest nearby. Whisper one line: We're still us. Notice any softening—yours or theirs.

    2.   Scent & Sun Ritual

For one week, keep a small item with the departed companion's scent in a quiet spot. Each morning, open blinds to let a square of sun reach it. Sit with your surviving pet in that light for a minute. Let warmth be a language.

3. Three-Anchor Walk

On your next walk (or indoor play for cats), name three anchors aloud: Time (what hour it is), Place (where you are), Together (who is with you). This simple naming reassures both nervous systems: we are oriented; we belong.

4. Memory Box, Living Box

Create two boxes. Into the Memory Box, place a photo, tag, note. Into the Living Box, place a new toy, a puzzle, a feather wand. Each evening, honor the memory; then play five minutes. Past and present, hand in paw.

5. Gentle Gate for New Love

If considering a new pet, light a candle and ask aloud: What kind of heartbeat would bless this house? Write three qualities (gentle, playful, calm). When the time comes, use these as your compass. Invite slowly, welcome widely, compare never.

Chapter 10: Soul Companions Forever
Love That Does Not End

The bond we form with our animal companions is not only an earthly connection—it is a soul agreement that stretches beyond lifetimes. The gentle gaze of a dog, the steady purr of a cat, the song of a bird, or the quiet watchfulness of a rabbit are not random moments of affection; they are spiritual encounters, teaching us what love without conditions feels like. Many traditions affirm this truth: our pets are not just creatures in our care, but guides, healers, and eternal companions who walk beside us in ways both visible and unseen.

When a beloved animal dies, we do not simply lose a pet—we step into a continuum of relationship that transforms form but never ends. The lessons they taught, the love they offered, and the presence they embodied become woven into our being. Through grief, we discover that their companionship does not vanish; it evolves into a subtler, enduring presence—what some call an eternal echo.

Soul Contracts: Agreements of the Heart

Spiritual teachers often speak of soul contracts—agreements made before birth between souls who choose to meet in this life for mutual growth. These contracts are not written in ink but in energy, intention, and love. Pets, in this view, arrive as part of these contracts, embodying specific lessons and healing tasks.

Mirror and teacher: Pets often mirror their human's energy—restlessness, calm, anxiety, or joy—so that we may recognize our own states and learn to transform them.

Healing partners: A dog who soothes a veteran's trauma or a cat who curls beside a grieving widow may be fulfilling a sacred assignment: to heal wounds that no human could reach.

Living reminders: By insisting on play, food, walks, and routine, pets teach balance—reminding us that bodies, joy, and presence matter as much as achievement.

Soul contracts affirm that our pets are not random visitors, but intentional companions sent to help us evolve.

Teachers of Unconditional Love

The deepest lesson pets impart is also the simplest: love

without judgment. A dog greets us with the same joy whether we return from work triumphant or defeated. A cat sits on our lap not because we performed well but because we are warm and safe. This constancy reveals the possibility of a love that is not transactional, not conditional, not earned, a love that is simply given.

Through their eyes, we learn:

Presence is enough: We are not loved for our success or status but for our being.

Forgiveness is natural: A scolded pet forgets the next moment and returns with tail wagging.

Joy is accessible: A stick, a sunbeam, a cardboard box—happiness can be simple.

To live what they model is to walk closer to the Divine.

Emotional and Spiritual Healing Through Companionship

Many people can trace their healing journey back to the steady presence of a pet. Survivors of trauma speak of nights endured only because a warm body pressed against theirs. Children who stutter find courage in reading aloud to a patient dog. Isolated elders rediscover laughter in the antics of a cat.

The healing they offer is not merely emotional but deeply energetic. Their nervous systems sync with ours; their calm lowers our heart rate; their affection releases oxytocin, bathing both species in trust and belonging. In silence, they communicate: You are safe. You are loved. Keep going.

Guidance and Intuition: Pets as Spiritual Guides

Beyond affection, pets often act as spirit guides in fur, feather, or scale. They sense storms before they come, illnesses before they're diagnosed, moods before they're admitted. Some stand at doors or windows as if alert to unseen presences; others dream with paws twitching, as if walking with us in realms beyond waking.

Even after death, many report their pets continue guiding them:

    A dream where the pet appears healthy and luminous, delivering reassurance.

    A sudden nudge felt at the ankle, though no body is there.

    A butterfly or bird showing up at uncanny moments, evoking their companion.

These are not illusions but messages: reminders that the

soul's bond is not broken.

Life Lessons from Soul Companions

Every animal teaches in their own way. A parrot

insists on voice, reminding us to speak our truth. A horse models strength married to gentleness. A rabbit teaches patience and gentleness in approach. Collectively, their lessons include:

Patience: Training, healing, and bonding all require time.

Boundaries: An anxious pet shows us the necessity of safe space and respect.

Responsibility: Daily care fosters discipline, presence, and accountability.

Grief and acceptance: Their shorter lifespans teach us to love fully despite inevitable partings.

Each lesson ripens the human soul.

Continuing Bonds Beyond Death

One of the most healing shifts in grief research is the concept of continuing bonds. Instead of urging people to "move on," it honors that the relationship continues in transformed ways:

Stories and memories: Telling their tales keeps their essence alive.

Memorials and rituals: Lighting a candle, planting a tree, or creating a memory box honors the bond.

Acts of service: Volunteering or donating in their name transforms grief into legacy.

Inner dialogue: Speaking to them in prayer or meditation, feeling their presence, listening for guidance.

In this light, death is not an erasure but a transition to a new form of relationship.

Growth in the Wake of Loss: Post-Traumatic Growth

The death of a beloved pet shatters routines, hearts, and identities. Yet many emerge changed in ways that surprise them—what psychologists call post-traumatic growth (PTG).

Resilience: Surviving "soul-crushing grief" proves an inner strength one did not know was there.

Appreciation: Life feels sharper, days more precious, relationships more vital.

Empathy: Having suffered, we become gentler toward others who grieve.

Purpose: Some channel their love into new missions—rescue work, writing, advocacy, or mentoring.

Spiritual depth: Reflection on death expands our philosophy, reminding us of interconnectedness and divine mystery.

Grief, though searing, becomes alchemical—turning loss into wisdom.

The Eternal Echo

In the quiet after loss, it may seem the world has gone dim. But if you listen differently, you will notice: a rhythm remains. The pawsteps may be gone, but the heart remembers the cadence. This is the eternal echo—the vibration of love that once shared space and now shares spirit. It is not fantasy; it is the way memory, biology, and spirit conspire to prove that love is not erasable.

Pets as soul companions remind us: love is eternal, and we are never truly alone. Their lessons endure, their presence lingers, and their guidance whispers through the fabric of our days. To remember them is to walk with them still.

Reflective Summary

Soul Companions Forever is not a slogan but a lived reality: the bond between human and animal is spiritual, intentional, and enduring. Through soul contracts, pets arrive as healers, mirrors, teachers, and guides. They embody unconditional love, stabilize our emotions, and offer intuitive wisdom. Their deaths, while devastating, are also thresholds to continuing bonds—through memory, ritual, and spiritual presence.

Grief, when faced with openness, becomes transformative. It cultivates resilience, deepens appreciation for life, expands empathy, clarifies purpose, and enriches spiritual understanding. To lose a pet is to suffer, but also to be reshaped into someone more tender, awake, and connected. In this way, pets continue to guide us even from beyond the veil, ensuring their love remains woven into our growth.

Their echo is eternal, and their companionship—forever.

Meditative Reflections

1. The Candle and the Collar (5 minutes)

Place your pet's collar or photo beside a lit candle. Breathe deeply, and whisper: Thank you for your love. Continue guiding me. Close your eyes, and imagine them sitting peacefully by your side, whole and free.

2. Walking With Memory

On a familiar walk, pause at three spots your pet loved. At each, say one word of gratitude (joy, comfort, loyalty). Feel the bond as a thread tying past to present.

3. Hand to Heart Prayer

Place your palm on your heart. Say aloud: The love between us is eternal. I carry you here. Stay for three breaths, sensing warmth spread outward.

4. The Eternal Echo Journal

Each week, write one lesson your pet taught you—patience, play, presence. Reflect on how you lived that lesson during the week. Over time, you'll see their wisdom woven into your life.

5. Continuing Bonds Ritual

Once a month, perform a simple act in their name—feed strays, donate to a shelter, light a candle, or tell a favorite story. Say: This is for you. We are still connected.

Chapter 11: The Cosmic Ark

The Old Story Sailing into the Future

Every culture keeps, somewhere in its memory, a story about waters rising and a vessel built in haste—an ark, a chest, a reed boat. Inside: breath, hooves, feathers, seeds; outside: wind and water and the long wait for a new world. Whether told around desert fires or written in sacred scrolls, the deeper message is the same: humans do not cross thresholds alone. We move through catastrophe and creation with the animal kingdom, not apart from it. That is the image behind the metaphor of the Cosmic Ark—a vessel as large as time itself, carrying our intertwined destinies from ancient nights to the neon now.

The Cosmic Ark is not a single ship; it is a continuum. It began when wary wolves drew closer to the edge of human camps and we, equally wary, tossed scraps to the dark. It continued as cats learned granaries, horses learned the arc of battle and plow, and pigeons learned the sky's postal routes. It is sailing still each time a therapy dog calms a shivering child, each time a lonely elder laughs at a cat's sovereign mischief, each time a conservation team releases a rehabilitated hawk back to wind. We are co-voyagers. We are co-authors. We are, at our best, co-guardians.

Humanity's Shared Journey with Animals

Coevolution: The First Passengers

Long before farms and city walls, a quiet bargain formed. The human niche promised food, fire, and shelter; in return, animals offered keen senses, strength, and—eventually—friendship. From the ashes of shared campsites rose a mutualistic alliance that shaped both species. Humans gained early warning systems, hunting partners, warmth, and meaning; animals gained stability and a new ecological opportunity. Over millennia, our bodies and brains co-adapted. We learned to read ears and eyes; they learned to read our faces and hands. The ancient deal was not only survival—it was the beginning of companionship.

Work, Survival, Story

Animals became force multipliers: oxen pressed earth into agriculture, horses stitched far distances into empires, pigeons outsourced messages to the wind. Cats patrolled granaries, dogs guarded thresholds, reindeer mapped the snows. But alongside work, animals entered myth: lions as courage, elephants as wisdom, cranes as longevity, dolphins as rescue, ravens as prophecy. They populated our imagination not as props but as symbols pointing to virtues we craved and vices we feared.

Scientific and Therapeutic Partners

In laboratories and clinics, animals have helped us decode genetics and invent medicine; in counseling rooms and hospital wards, they help us heal what science alone cannot touch. The dog beside a veteran in a crowded store; the cat that coaxes a conversation from a depressed teenager; the horse that teaches a boundary to someone who never had one—animal-assisted therapy is the ark docking at our most human harbors.

The Modern Ark: Love, Law, and Responsibility

We no longer rely on animals for daily survival the way our ancestors did; grocery stores replaced foraging, tractors replaced teams. Yet our bond did not diminish—it deepened. Pets moved from yard to couch to bed to family status. Laws shifted to protect them; shelters evolved from holding pens to adoption hubs that recognize personality and welfare. We discovered what we already felt: that animals experience not only hunger and fear, but curiosity, play, preference, and attachment.

With that awareness came responsibility. The conversation widened to welfare, rights, and conservation. We asked: What do we owe the creatures whose bodies labor for our comfort? How do we protect the wild kin whose habitats our choices erase? The Cosmic Ark in the twenty-first century is less about surviving a flood than preventing one: rising seas of extinction, climate displacement, and moral indifference.

In the modern ark, animals are cherished companions, therapeutic partners, co-workers, and keystone beings within ecosystems. We are still learning how to be worthy shipmates.

Pets as Spiritual Crew: Teachers, Healers, Guides

Within this ark, pets are not cargo. They are crew—teachers, healers, navigators of both our outer and inner seas.

Teachers

Unconditional love and acceptance: They love beyond our résumés and mistakes, teaching us to love without ledger books.

Presence: Their joy in a sunbeam, a walk, a cardboard box instructs us in mindfulness.

Patience and forgiveness: They reset to affection faster than we do, modeling the liberation of letting go.

Empathy and compassion: Caring daily for another being trains the heart to look outward and respond.

Healers and Guides

Emotional regulation: Petting releases oxytocin, calming stormy physiology; their steady presence entrains our hearts toward coherence.

Spiritual protection and intuition: Across cultures, animals are guardians at thresholds—sensing danger, alerting us, sitting vigil when we cannot sleep.

Soul contracts: Many intuit a sacred choreography: certain animals arrive exactly when we need them most, to help us heal trauma or change course.

The spiritual perspective does not inflate pets into angels nor deflate them into property. It names the truth we feel: our growth is intertwined with theirs. They help us practice the world we long to live in—one of kindness, responsibility, and reverence.

Ethics on Open Water: From Ownership to Stewardship

To sail well together requires ethics that keep pace with affection and knowledge.

Welfare: Enrichment, space, social needs, medical care—love operationalized.

Consent and boundaries: Learning to read a cat's "enough," a dog's stress signals, a horse's body language honors personhood-in-practice, even if the law lags.

Conservation: Domestic love must widen into wild mercy—habitat protection, humane policies, respect for indigenous knowledge about non-human kin.

The ark asks for a new word beyond ownership: stewardship—not dominion, not sentimentality, but mutual flourishing.

The Mystical Future: Bridges of Mind and Law

What might the Cosmic Ark become if we dared to sail by stars we've barely named?

Shared Consciousness and Interspecies Translation

Advances in AI and machine learning are already decoding patterns in whale song, birdsong, and primate calls. Imagine tools that translate basic needs and feelings—hunger, pain, play, fear—then graduate to context, preference, and rudimentary concepts. The first "two-way" bridges will likely be clunky, partial, and astonishing. Real-time stress interpretation could elevate welfare; feedback loops could refine animal-assisted therapies to respect the animal's needs as much as the humans.

These bridges would press a hard, beautiful question: if we can understand more of what animals mean, can we continue to treat them as things? The answer would ripple through ethics, education, and law.

Animal Personhood and the "One Planet" Ethos

As evidence of sentience, emotion, and problem-solving mounts—and communication improves—societies may move toward forms of legal personhood for certain species or contexts. Not human equivalence, but recognized standing: the right not to be tortured, the right to habitat, the right to representation in decisions that determine survival. This shift could seed a broader One Planet mindset: one biosphere, many minds, shared fate. Human exceptionalism gives way to human responsibility.

New Roles in a Shared Future

Technology partners: Animals participating—by consent-aware design—in therapeutic programs with biofeedback that protects their stress thresholds.

Conservation collaborators: Community science with respectful animal tracking that prioritizes animal agency and ecosystem health.

Spiritual expansion: As we learn to listen across species, theology and philosophy may rediscover an old truth with new language: spirit is not a human monopoly.

In this mystical future, the ark is a university of love and consciousness. We are students as much as captains.

Practices for Ark-Worthy Living (Right Now)

The Cosmic Ark is not only a vision; it is a daily practice:

1. **Attention as devotion:** Learn your companion's signals. Let their comfort, not convenience, set the boundary.

2. **Enrichment as ethics:** Boredom is suffering. Offer puzzles, perches, scent walks, training games—species-appropriate joy.

3. **Choice as dignity**: Build in micro-choices—approach or not, retreat space, training with consent cues.

4. **Community as lifeboat**: Support shelters, foster, volunteer, donate. Advocate for humane policy.

5. **Wild mercy**: Plant native, reduce plastic, vote for habitat, keep cats indoors or in catios, leash near nesting areas—small acts, real impact.

6. **Ritual and remembrance**: Honor the dead; support the living. Grief matured into stewardship is legacy.

Each act is a plank in the ark.

Navigating Awe: Why This Journey Matters

Awe is not decoration; it is orientation. Awe tells us where we stand in the order of things—small, responsible, connected. When a dog meets your eyes and you both understand the next right thing; when a whale breaches and the sea writes an exclamation into the sky; when a fox steps out at dusk and the world holds its breath—you are looking at cosmic curriculum. The lesson is plain and limitless: we belong to one another.

The ark is not only Noah's story. It is our story—the long canoe of kinship where paws and hands share oars. We will survive, and more than survive, together—or not at all.

Reflective Summary

The Cosmic Ark reframes our history with animals as a shared voyage across eras: from coevolution and utility to companionship, therapy, and spiritual kinship. Animals have labored beside us, populated our myths, and stabilized our nervous systems; today they are family, healers, and partners whose welfare and agency demand thoughtful ethics. Within this ark, pets are spiritual crew—teachers of presence and forgiveness, healers of trauma, and guides appointed by love (what many name soul contracts).

Looking forward, technology may build bridges of understanding that compel legal and moral evolution—toward forms of animal personhood and a One Planet ethos. In such a future, animals are not property but participants, and the ark becomes a school of shared consciousness and reverence. Right now, we embody this vision through daily stewardship—attention, enrichment, choice, community, wild mercy, and ritual. The through-line from flood myth to tomorrow's lab is simple and sacred: our fates are interwoven. To honor that truth is to steer the ark wisely.

Meditative Reflections

1.   Ark Inventory (5 minutes)

List the animals who have shaped you—past and present. For each, write one lesson (patience, courage, joy). Close by whispering: Thank you for your passage with me.

2.   One Planet Breath

Inhale: We belong. Exhale: We protect. Repeat for ten breaths, visualizing your breath flowing through forests, oceans, cities, and back to your heart. Let responsibility feel like devotion.

3.   Consent Check

Before touch or play, pause and observe your pet's cues: soft eyes, loose body, eager approach—or avoidance, yawning, turning away. If invited, proceed; if not, honor the no. Say aloud: Your yes matters.

4.   Wild Mercy Walk

Take a walk dedicated to non-human neighbors. Pick up trash, notice bird calls, step lightly around insects. Promise one practical change (native plant, less plastic, safer window decals). Seal it by touching a tree: We are crew.

5. Future Bridge Intention

Light a candle and imagine a world where we understand animals better—through intuition, study, or technology. Ask, what small bridge can I build this week? (A training game, a donation, a letter to a representative.) Do it. Let vision become plank.

Chapter 12: Forever Present

The Eternal Echo of Love

When a beloved pet passes, the silence can feel deafening—the absence of paws on the floor, the missing warmth pressed against your side, the routines abruptly broken. Yet even in this absence, something remains. The love shared does not vanish; it becomes an eternal echo that continues to shape and comfort us. This echo is the lasting resonance of unconditional love, woven into memory, body, and spirit.

Grief reminds us of love's depth. To mourn deeply is to have loved profoundly. While grief stings, it also testifies to the joy, stability, and companionship a pet gave. Over time, sorrow bends toward gratitude. The pain softens into memory, and memory matures into presence. Pets may leave the physical world, but they are forever present in the heart.

Honoring the Eternal Echo

One of the most healing steps after loss is to memorialize the pet—to give form to the love that remains. Rituals and symbols transform grief into continuity.

Memorial spaces: A corner with their photo, collar, or favorite toy becomes a sacred site for remembrance.

Tributes in words: Writing a letter or journal entry allows unspoken gratitude, regrets, and love to flow freely.

Living memorials: Planting a tree, a rose bush, or a patch of wildflowers ensures that their life blossoms into beauty long after their passing.

Keepsakes: Paw-print jewelry, custom portraits, or engraved urns become tangible reminders of an invisible bond.

Communal ceremonies: Inviting friends or family to share memories affirms that the pet's life was cherished and meaningful.

Memorials do not keep us trapped in grief; they transform absence into visible presence, reminding us that what we love becomes part of us.

Messages of Comfort

When grief feels unbearable, words can become lifelines. Quotes, poems, and prayers distill wisdom into compact comfort:

> "What we have once enjoyed we can never lose; all that we love deeply becomes a part of us." — Helen Keller

> "How lucky I am to have something that makes saying goodbye so hard." — A.A. Milne, Winnie the Pooh

Such words remind us that grief is not the end of love—it is love persisting, reshaped. They also normalize sorrow, validating that pet grief is not "too much," but a natural reflection of a sacred bond.

Living Forward with Gratitude

To live forward after loss is not to abandon grief but to walk with it differently. Gratitude becomes the bridge.

Accept That Love Never Ends

The pain of absence is the measure of how deeply we loved. When we shift from "they are gone" to "they are part of me now," grief begins to integrate.

Acknowledge Lasting Influence

Pets leave us changed. They may have taught patience, forgiveness, humor, or presence. Recognizing these lessons allows us to live as their legacy.

Recognize the Validity of Pet Grief

Dismissive comments like "it was just a pet" miss the truth: pets are family. Their loss destabilizes daily rhythms and emotional anchors. Naming the grief as valid restores dignity to the mourner and honors the role the pet played.

Ways to Live with Gratitude

Create a memorial: Memory boxes, gardens, portraits, or jewelry keep their presence tactile and close.

Channel grief into action: Volunteer at a shelter, foster an animal, or donate in your pet's name. These acts expand love outward, turning sorrow into blessing.

Incorporate memory into daily life: Continue walking their favorite route, keep a chair empty in their honor, or light a candle at mealtime.

Believe in eternal connection: The Rainbow Bridge, reincarnation, or the idea of soul contracts—all offer comfort that bonds endure beyond the veil.

Gratitude shifts loss from paralysis into purpose. It does not erase grief, but it transforms it into something livable and luminous.

The Rainbow Bridge

Perhaps no story has comforted more grieving hearts than the legend of the Rainbow Bridge. Written as a poem in the 1980s, it envisions a meadow where pets wait, healthy and joyful, free from pain. They linger, but they are not complete. They miss their human.

The reunion comes when the human dies. From across the meadow, pet and person see each other again. With joyous recognition, they run to meet. No more separation, no more loss—only reunion. Together, they cross the bridge into eternity.

This vision may not be dogma, but it is medicine: a balm for the aching heart. It paints loss not as ending but as delay, not as absence but as interval. For children and adults alike, the Rainbow Bridge gives grief a horizon of hope.

Religious and Spiritual Perspectives

Faith traditions wrestle with the question: Do animals have souls? Answers vary, but the yearning is universal.

Christianity: Classical theology often denied eternal souls to animals, yet modern voices (from C.S. Lewis to Billy Graham) speak of a renewed creation where animals share heaven. Romans 8 and Isaiah 11 describe creation redeemed, lions beside lambs.

Judaism: Rabbinic thought rarely affirms animal afterlife, yet some Hasidic traditions imagine souls continuing, sometimes even reincarnating.

Islam: Animals are considered perpetual worshipers of God. Some interpretations envision them judged and dissolved, others comfort that pets may accompany loved humans into paradise.

Eastern traditions: Hinduism, Buddhism, and Jainism affirm animal souls within samsara, reincarnating according to karma. Compassion toward animals is seen as vital to liberation.

Mystical perspectives: Theosophy and Spiritualism suggest animals share in soul evolution, perhaps reincarnating within soul families across lifetimes.

Across traditions, one theme repeats: animals are not disposable. They are threads in the eternal fabric of creation, and their destiny is tied to ours.

The Psychological Comfort of Reunion

Even beyond faith, reunion stories serve a vital psychological role.

Coping with loss: Narratives like the Rainbow Bridge give grief a positive image to hold.

Meaning-making: They affirm that love mattered and continues.

Relief from guilt: Knowing the pet is pain-free allows owners to soften regrets, especially after euthanasia.

Hope for reunion: Hope itself becomes healing, reminding us that love has no expiration date.

Grief demands meaning. Reunion narratives offer just that—a way to reconcile love's endurance with death's reality.

Reflective Summary

Forever Present affirms that the death of a beloved pet does not end the bond; it transforms it. Through

memorials, words of comfort, and daily acts of remembrance, grief matures into gratitude. Stories like the Rainbow Bridge, along with religious and spiritual traditions, assure us that pets remain part of the eternal tapestry of love.

Living forward with gratitude means integrating their presence into memory, action, and hope. Whether through creating memorials, volunteering, telling stories, or simply carrying their lessons into daily life, we continue the relationship in a new form. The grief we feel is the echo of love, and that echo is proof: love is never lost. Love is forever present.

Meditative Reflections

    1.   The Candle of Presence

Light a candle in your pet's honor. As it burns, whisper three words they taught you (such as joy, loyalty, forgiveness). Imagine these qualities glowing within you.

    2.   Rainbow Bridge Visualization

Close your eyes and imagine your pet restored to perfect health, running across a field. See them pause, look back at you with love, and then continue joyfully. Feel peace in knowing reunion awaits.

    3.   Gratitude Journal

Each evening for a week, write one happy memory of your pet. Let sorrow transform into thankfulness, building a treasury of love.

4.   Living Legacy

Do one small act of kindness in your pet's name—feeding strays, donating food, comforting another mourner. Say aloud: This is for you. Your love continues through me.

5.   Silent Presence

Sit quietly with your eyes closed. Feel your breath rise and fall. Place a hand on your heart and imagine their heartbeat within yours. Rest in the eternal echo of love.

Epilogue: The Eternal Echo

The Blessing of Companionship Beyond Time

In every paw print, in every feather, in every soft breath that once shared our world, there remains an echo. The chapters of this section have carried us through grief's silence, memory's embrace, and the soul's discovery that love is never broken by death. Pets are not only companions for a season; they are soul travelers, entrusted to us for a time, and entrusted with us forever.

The Eternal Echo reminds us that every bond we form is inscribed in the fabric of the universe. Through soul contracts, our pets arrive to teach, to heal, to protect, and to love without conditions. When their bodies fall away, their essence remains—woven into the pulse of our days and the shaping of our hearts. Their lessons ripple forward: patience, forgiveness, joy in simple things, compassion that reaches beyond species.

The ark of companionship sails on. Some of our beloveds may return to us in new forms, others wait at the threshold of the Rainbow Bridge, and still others guide us from unseen realms. Whether through dreams, synchronicities, or the quiet warmth we feel in memory, their presence abides. They are not gone; they are forever present.

And so, we bless this journey. May we walk it with reverence, gratitude, and hope:

With reverence, for the sacredness of every creature's life and the mystery of our shared path.

With gratitude, for the joy, healing, and companionship our pets have given us.

With hope, for the day when reunion comes—whether across a meadow of eternal light, or in the quiet recognition of their spirit within our own.

The Eternal Echo is love's promise: what is given in love is never lost. What has been shared continues. And as we continue our journey, we do so not alone, but always accompanied by those who have loved us with fur, feather, scale, or song.

Benediction for Cody and Chloe

–MysticSojourn66–

In silken white, two souls drew near,
With laughter bright and hearts sincere.
Their gentle eyes, their tender way,
Turned ordinary nights to day.

Through quiet walks and joyful play,
They taught that love need not repay.
No judgment held, no burden stayed,
Just loyalty that never swayed.

When silence fell, their spirits rose,
Two kindred flames the cosmos chose.
Though paws grew still, their essence sings,
In whispered winds and angel wings.

Cody's gaze, a steady star,
Chloe's joy still felt afar.
Together woven in the thread,
Of love that lives beyond the dead.

ARWIN VALENCIA, MD

Their presence lingers, soft and true,
In every dawn, in skies of blue.
A sacred bond that will not sever,
For love endures, and lives forever.

So, rest, dear friends, in heaven's light,
Your echoes guard each passing night.
Until the bridge we cross anew,
My heart is whole—because of you.

About the Author

Arwin M. Valencia, MD is a physician, writer, and lifelong lover of animals whose heart has been profoundly shaped by the unconditional companionship of his beloved Coton de Tuléar dogs, Cody and Chloe. As a neonatologist, he has spent decades at the threshold of life, witnessing its fragility, resilience, and mystery. His professional journey caring for the most vulnerable lives has deepened his reverence for all living beings and sharpened his awareness of the sacred bond between humans and animals.

Blending medical insight with spiritual reflection, Dr. Valencia writes with compassion about grief, healing, and the eternal nature of love. Forever Present was born from personal loss, but also from profound gratitude—for the joy, loyalty, and wisdom that pets bring into our lives. Through this book, he hopes to bring comfort to those who mourn and to honor the truth that our pets are never "just animals," but soul companions whose presence echoes forever in our hearts.